Labels Belong on Jars

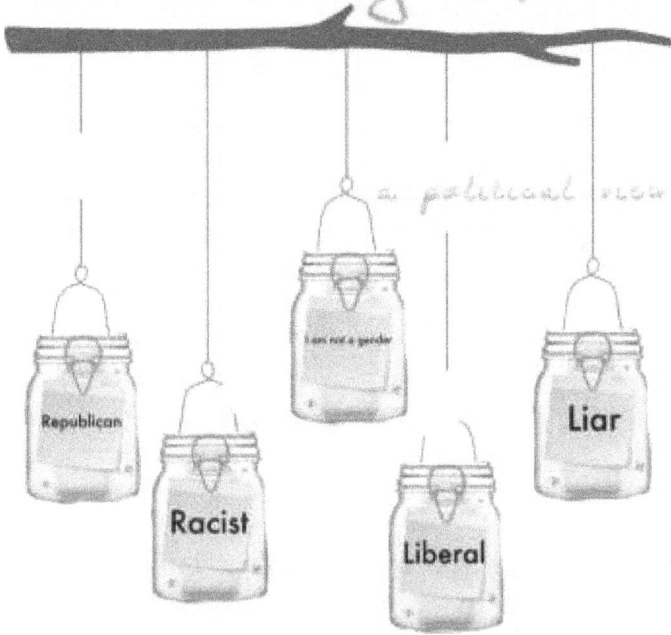

a political view

i am not a gender

Republican

Racist

Liberal

Liar

Mother, Businesswomen, Innovator, Political Surrogate, Provocateur & World Traveler

Maria Jay LoRicco, MSW

ISBN: 978-1-952263-67-5

Dedication

I want to dedicate this book to my father, Richard A. LoRicco, and my grandfather Anthony LoRicco.

About the Author

Maria LoRicco is a developer of chemical-free, farm to pouch vegetable food products. She thinks that food should be valued for nutrition and serve a purpose for good health. She has one patent and nine trademarks, all self-issued. She is a devoted activist for nutrition, recycling, two-tier taxpayer, right to life, and school and healthcare choice. She has been a traveler all her life from unusual trips as a teenager to USSR when it became Russia to Uganda, Africa. She received a Bachelor of Science degree in Hotel and Restaurant Management, and its application has been dedicated to a 30year banquet business. Prior to that, she received a B.S. in Political Science and prelaw.

After she gave birth to her son, she began a nanny agency called Care Bears, where she lived in Hillsboro Beach, Florida. She practiced both residential and commercial Real Estate. She moved to the East Coast while pursuing a Master of Social Services degree in Manhattan, New York. She wrote as an advocate for special education for her son's elementary school newsletter. She was a political liaison for Concerned Women for America, Committee spokesperson for The League of Women Voters Recycling, voter's registration, and business development in the community of Westport, Connecticut, and a volunteer for countless political campaigns. Her goal is efficiency. She lives in a traditional two-story home with a vegetable and flower garden. She shares her home with her son, Sky, and his model girlfriend, Talisa. Enjoying good food and engaging discussions with her family of entrepreneurs.

Prior to that, she received a B.S. in Political Science and prelaw. After she gave birth to her son, she began a nanny agency called Care Bears, where she lived in Hillsboro Beach, Florida. She practiced both residential and commercial Real Estate. She moved to the East Coast while pursuing a Master of Social Services degree in Manhattan, New York. She wrote as an advocate for special education for her son's elementary school newsletter. She was a political liaison for Concerned Women for America, Committee spokesperson for The League of Women Voters Recycling, voter's registration, and business development in the community of Westport, Connecticut, and a volunteer for countless political campaigns. Her goal is efficiency. She lives in a traditional two-story home with a vegetable and flower garden. She shares her home with her son, Sky, and his model girlfriend, Talisa. Enjoying good food and engaging discussions with her family of entrepreneurs.

Maria also day trades with her son and shares caring for his two Siamese cats Bali and Tom, along with Tootsie a 20 lbs bipooh. To her, celebrating a simple life is quite a joy. She no longer makes life happen. She has mastered getting wiser and lets life happen! She spent the last twelve years in her hometown running the food manufacturing business she founded, GotMeals, LLC. A regimen of exercising outdoors including one of her favorite activities spent running, tennis with friends, bicycling or kayaking at her home in Deerfield Beach or the Harbor two blocks from her Connecticut home.

Acknowledgment

I grew up the youngest child in an extended family that was exclusively male (not counting me). My father was the breadwinner for the family, as was the traditional model, and as such, he was seldom present for my mother. Her role, by contrast, was to be the glue that held the family together – the nurturer, the healer, the emotional support.

My father was removed from the day-to-day functioning of family life. His role was to preside over family dinners, to absorb the news of the day from his children and his wife, and to offer judgments about what had taken place and what was to be done about it.

That traditional family structure was what nurtured me when I was a young girl – and what I rebelled against when I grew older and became increasingly aware of the big world beyond the cloistered cocoon world inside our family home. I sometimes compared my life parallel to Buddha sheltered from the problems of the world – until he became empowered to change his circumstances. I attended elementary school in the 1970s. That was when I had my first run-in with authority – and with corruption. My friend

Chrissy grew up across the street from us. I wanted to be a cheerleader for our school more than anything else in the world. I had the talent and the background and the ballet classes and was a natural fit with all the skills and qualifications to make the perfect cheerleader. Chrissy, by contrast, had not a modicum of the dance talent or passion that I had. But she did have one thing that I did not have: connections. Chrissy's cousin, Ann, was the captain of the cheerleading squad. That meant Chrissy was in, and I was out.

This may have been my first real taste of failure and my first real confrontation with corruption – or reality if you prefer. And I rebelled against it – because it was so unfair, but even more than that, because it was politics and we were just children.

A few years later, I entered high school — an expensive private Catholic girls' high school. Even among that relative affluence, I stood out as kind of a glitzy girl — I had expensive jewelry. All the girls wore uniforms, of course, but our uniforms were not exactly uniform. My clothes were neatly pressed and tailored. As good Catholic girls, our skirts were supposed to fall below the knee. Mine, was fashionable above the knee – which was not lost on Father Doherty, the head chaplain, who pulled me aside and said, "You know, Maria, of all the girls I have taught at this school, you're the only girl whose underwear I never saw – and many do not wear anything under the uniform..." (What would happen if that remark was made in our contemporary #MeToo environment?).

Who is protected innocence or the predator? I may have a man like that in the bathroom according to present sexual harassment standards. Just the same I was too young to know other than the creepiness of the conversation that caused me to bolt. All the girls bragged of their friendship with the priest; I simply was confused: Was he complimenting me that I was more sophisticated than the other girls? Being raised in a rigid environment, I was taught never to go out of the house without underwear and to keep my knees together and sit like a lady. Coincidentally the benefits of my Sicilian upbringing may have come in handy.

That was one of my first object lessons in the harsh reality that, if you choose to stand out from your peers, you're going to have to accept and prepared to cope with the backlash that will follow. So that was a valuable life lesson to blend.

The double standards seemed to contradict my worldview. Mrs. Ellen Gann, the Spanish teacher, jibed at me, "Candy, you're an airhead." Aren't teachers supposed to encourage their students? At the senior prom, I was set up by the entire academic receiving line as they enjoyed the pleasure of meeting me with the police as I pulled up to the banquet facility. Pretty radical for the 1980s, I drove my prom date!

One spring break Mom and I journeyed to Bermuda, where I met a boy whose mom and dad flew him to the local airport in our town, New Haven, for the prom. There was a pre-party at Kim's house in Stratford, CT. I volunteered to bring the booze to the after-party; it was stashed in the back seat behind the driver's seat. The police and school officials insisted that my car be searched. I refused to comply. The flashlights were pulled out from the side of the officer's holster.

I was walking around the car, shining the bright light in search of drugs and alcohol. I felt like I killed someone and was concealing a dead body. Whoever put the alcohol in my car covered it with a blanket. The officer ordered me to open the trunk. "No – it is not my car," I replied. "Call home and ask your parents," he ordered. "We will ask their permission to search their car, and then you're not going inside to the prom." I protested, "If I am not going inside, then you are going to reimburse me for my prom tickets."

I stood up to those bullies, and since no one answered my phone call home, the officers decided there was nothing suspicious. The administration received me with a contradiction of hospitality. Then there was Donna Ragizino, who fixed Sue Whaleon up with my original date, Mark. I met him at Donna's family's boat during the summer. When I found the boy from Massachusetts in Bermuda to replace the mean conspiracy to prevent me from attending the prom, I relished walking into the prom with the most handsome mystery guy.

I graduated from elementary and high school, the most popular in my class, and the best dressed. Seeing how everyone was friendly to my face but then talked behind my back, I no longer paid attention to them. I knew who could be trusted, and I had no time for insincerities. I went to college in Florida with my father's best friend's son, Vinny. When Vinny went to rehab, my father insisted I come back home to go to the school where I grew up, New Haven,

Connecticut. Thanks to my father's intervention, the lack of tuition payment brought college in Florida to an abrupt halt. I came home for the summer and was never allowed to go back to as much as collect my belongings. I rebelled against my father's strictures. I wanted to learn hotel management, so I could someday take over that part of my father's business.

Had I remained in a specific vocation, I would not have the classical strong traditional liberal-arts approach to know political systems, philosophy, law, and economics. Losing my personal effects, never saying goodbye to friends, seemed cruel. My world ended; my friend Michael saw me through the ambiguities of moving on his advice was, "you are only cutting off your nose to spite your face." I fell in love with his friend Peter.

We even went to Albertus Magnus College together. We lived together at his family's beach home in Milford, Connecticut. I loved attending auctions, and similarly, he grew up attending auctions with his family. My Dad was his Dad's attorney, where many conversations consisted of comparing oriental carpets from auctions. I decorate the beach house, and Peter bought a brand-new baby blue

Cadillac, Biarritz, with a white leather interior, with a sunroof! Family, friends, and pursuing our dreams seemed like I was insulated from the social climb of pretentious friends. My traditional family rejected my lifestyle and forbade me to live together with my boyfriend. I grew distant from them and decided I did not need them either. I learned to dance with the devil.

I confronted trying to save my boyfriend from a drug addiction believing in him when he promised, "I can stop." I stayed long after my trust had been broken. I wanted to have nothing to do with where he was going. I knew my goal would be compromised if I took him where I was along. There was no room for more dishonesty, and he made a choice easier after years of a tangled lie. The ultimatum was "You choose; it's either me or her (heroin)."

There are parts that I have to skip that may incriminate others even though the state of limitations precludes incrimination. The bloody clothes in the trunk probably would have forfeited my dreams. He was extradited from Amsterdam to serve a sentence for drug distribution. During those years, I had met the father of my son.

But for the glory of a 6lb.8oz. saving blessing, my son, Sky was born. I threw away the false life that protected me from the dreadful phony people in my life. I thank my son, SKY, for being born and the great man that whenever I reached out for fatherly support, he was there, Richard.

I became a Realtor in 1994, where we resided in Hillsboro Beach, Florida. Not being included in condominium meetings was the first experience with bureaucracy. I called the condominium board "Condo Comando's" Their group didn't include a consensus. The Board of Education operated similarly, moving posted meeting rooms without notifying all attendees. Kept out of an alternate view has insulated corrupt entities that only want elite rule. I came head-on with big bullies no better than big businesses camouflage as women health care providers or administration, i.e., Planned Parenthood and the School Superintendent, preventing me from coequally present educational enrichment workshops proving another side to the only message. I taught catechism at Saint Luke's Church in Westport, CT. During Sky's field trip, I was preparing a lesson for after school class. The parent who was a medical doctor noticed the Bible and curtly lectured that I was lucky she allowed me in her car.

The examining Board at Fordham University School of Social Services scalped me for limiting the schedule I had for extra assignments for the school. My Supervisor reprimanded me that my family life should not take priority over my work. As a social work provider, I thought where is their compassion, understanding, and care for children growing up with single mothers. Unless you were part of the problem, there was no hand up if you lifted yourself up, these atheist, single-minded dictators had an agenda get on board if you can go along with us. I could not look away.

Dinner parties intimidated, alienated, and ignored upon mentioning a political view that is not part of the cabal. I spent years feeling like I was green, but if it was not for the conditioning of being lied to, pandered to, and asymmetrically polarize for my beliefs, I might shrink and conform. I thank all the uncomfortable conversations, all the bullies, everyone who hates Gd, family, and will not include anyone who disagrees with their view because of you – I am telling the other side. A decorator for the Congresswomen told me he never let a Republican in his car and that I would be the first and last. I was happy to tell him I was independent. So much time passes from lifelong best friends as you travel through your 50's. On a recent trip from Beena's home in California to bring their son Christian back to school in Boston. My best friend and her husband James, headed to Nantucket before arriving in CT. to see family. She began to describe they attended an Indian Museum! Christopher Columbus is European Christian patriarchy, responsible for scalping the Indians and stealing this land from them. Revising history, because of his profile seems acceptable to certain Americans. Expunging the Explorer credentials, heroism, faith, and intelligence is insincere. The Indians themselves invented scalping live animals for material and food. The pilgrims came over with the greatest toy the Indians ever saw the revolver.

The tribes fought amongst themselves and skinned other tribal leaders to judicial and lawfully dominate land, possessions, and ideas. When the English man showed up with guns, they traded land for arms. They annihilated their enemies, set fire to dissenters, and preserved their tribal inheritance. Did civilized men look upon them as equals? Probably not... But tell both sides. It seems everyone for a price can be bought. Transparency is honorable. A clandestine hoax that promotes an ulterior motive is called an agenda. I will give you free goods if you vote for me. Is a disguise layered with the real intention few are willing to recognize? When turmoil and chaos lead us into destruction, the mechanism of suppression is the only victor.

Free money is a promise that causes anyone to accept "public assistance" to live from paycheck to paycheck. However, those very politicians entice voters, a false lure, pandering for an insincere vote. If society is to progress with equity, the standard of living that is attainable is for anyone willing to work hard and save money. Old money was made by understanding – to make money you need to save money, Benjamin Franklin said, "the greatest force in the universe was compound interest."

When we are young starting out with our first careers, there is a sacrifice to live frugally and save money that will benefit one's monetary future tenfold. Over a period of time without disturbing the principal investment, you can spend the profit on traveling freely, educate yourself freely, or have upward mobility. Alternatively, there is an income class under you who believes the lie that society can bear the burden to pay taxes. A false sense of security is misleading the group that is enticed to lean on the government social services instead of building a future. Doing anything you want is different from being anything you want. Do not allow an easy life of pleasure and doing what you want to suppress the drive to be anything you want to be. Will you try to see the other side after 200 years, break free because the lie can rob you of a financially independent future that is waiting for you to grab.

In keeping an open mind, we allow personal growth. The bullies and situations that cause the greatest angst taught me – through negative examples – to stand up to and eventually overcome them. Gratitude is itself Posterity!

"You will never know how much it cost the present generation to preserve your freedom! I hope you will make good use of it."

-John Adams

Preface

The sensation of accomplishment and achievement is incomparable. However, we can't always accomplish something without relentless effort. There are habits you need to develop an introspection that guides a sense of consciousness to actualize your goals. Optimizing the environment around you shapes your place in the world. Your awareness of mobilizing power is the tenacity through which you can create a lifestyle that you imagine with a lot of focus and the discipline to develop intentional thought. Determine habits that propel our environmental symbiosis, allows us to control positive thinking, and block negative energy.

Inevitably our personal development relies on identity, self-love, and the fortitude to be deterministic. Blaming people or organic hindrances is a cope out from facing the truth within ourselves. We cannot control the life we are born into, but we can control the people or influences that we allow into our space, whether physically in relationships or virtually, i.e., through media, academia, or the internet. Awareness of individual cost factors is assessed as a drain or gain to reaching one's potential. Situations and information are influencers that can either build us up or break us down; the decision remains ours as to who or what we choose to have our power. Protecting one's power is the key to self-love.

Maria LoRicco's book "Labels belong on Jars" is the perfect guide book to understand the impact environment plays and empower you to take control of the destiny you imagine. Grab a copy now and start working on shaping the environment you want today!

Contents

Page Left Blank Intentionally

Chapter 1
Break the mold

When was the last time you lied to someone? Maybe a few hours, a few days, a few weeks ago. We all lie sometimes. It is perfectly human. It doesn't really matter when you last lied, or to whom you lied to. The thing that matters most is why you lied. Often, it's for personal gain. There are white lies, too – lies we tell to fool ourselves or to avoid hurting another person's feelings. We are so inured to lying that, much of the time, we don't even bother to identify the reason why we lied.

I believe the factor that induces us to lie is the Fear of Not Being Validated By Others. When you are forced to confront the fact that you have failed an exam, didn't get the job or are rejected from a school, you begin at once to think about the excuses that you can use as a shield to justify your failure. The fear of not fulfilling the expectations of those around us is more powerful than that of failure itself.

Everything you've encountered in your life is a projection of your identity. A vast majority of people live their lives through the viewpoint of the people and life experiences that have influenced them. The new order is emerging. Advanced by COVID- 19, the weak have been purged by random elimination. Expressed by the term "weak" is the reference to immune-compromised deficiencies. Replacing vast numbers of elderly, diabetic, HIV positive, or chronic deficiencies with an "Apple" generation.

Millenniums and Generation Z familiar with robotic modalities impregnate erudite socialization. Society has emerged in a virtual world. Replaced are arbitrary thought, activities, work, and leisure. Life has become planned, and the precise schedule has mitigated the monotonous salutation "what are you doing today" replaced with "what's your schedule look like, Tuesday at 2 p.m."

The goddess of victory etymologically can be traced to 300 BC; her human nature is to win. That is not the complete reality of life. The Greek goddess of victory, whose name is Nike, served in the Greek Senate with her brothers, named Rivalry, Strength, and Force. Epistemologists waste efforts to disprove the translation of the logos, but the permanence of architecture, archaeologist carbon dating, and historical manuscripts during the reigns of kings are factual accounts that have proven conspiracy theories otherwise. Knowing our origin, humanity allows the individual to synthesis a connection to good and other natural forces.

The individual can best understand life is a dynamic that requires a road map of how best to live. Which sentinel will you be if Zeus asked you to reign in Olympus against the attack of the Titans? Throughout the Middle East, the oldest civilizations, there is only one true God, yet throughout civilization, there is a persistent fight of good and evil. The Bible tells us not to be lukewarm. Any side that demonizes or blames another side is causing damage to their personal growth.

To be accountable for oneself begins with replacing old ways with the maturity to improve, growing from our mistakes. To deny self-reliance, we blame circumstances or other people, and we then become an oppressor to others and ourselves. Complaining is self-destructive, but making a plan on how to tackle a goal is a process of self-actualization. Don't shoot the messenger comes from ancient prophets that delivered a divine message to their contemporaries only to fall upon deaf ears that were insulted to anger, refusing to open their heart, obey to turn from their debacle and believe.

Polarizing by calling labels such as racist, redneck, lesbian, rich, poor is self-sabotaging. That which we see in others is a mere reflection of ourselves.

Inclusion must embrace not demonize those whom we disagree with. In an effort to distance any group, one disagrees from belonging perpetuates disenfranchising that group or person. Avoiding a conversation reduces all thought to mindless intimidation. Advancing symbiotic respect includes equity of life. That is why the greatest crime is to snuff out life. That is a consensus of the civilized world. It is a crime punished by humanity that separates perpetrators who forcefully defy the human contract and harm another.

The Bible sees gossip as an abomination. The United States liable law protects against the slanderous act to punish those creating rivalry within society. A virtual world is emerging gone are the days of in-person doctor appointments, children's learning, live interviews, household shopping, exercise, and worship, which are replacing activities of leisure and work with planned schedules. The future is shaping for all to take part in a programmed robotic form of existence. Exemplified is a choice to be ruled or to be autonomously represented by choice between 50 States in America and what form of government each uniquely legislates by. The rise of the individual will play a vital role in choosing an environment coexisting with how one thinks and behaves.

The environment we are born into may be random, but the city and state that govern the way we express ourselves in adulthood are our choices. Recognizing we are free to live anywhere is a small liberty taken for granted and in many countries forbidden. Being the youngest child and the only female in a family of men, I grew up differently. I never conformed to the expectations of the group without finding a valid justification behind them.

It was not until I lived a single life, unmarried did I realize tradition is wiser. I am Maria LoRicco, a 55-year-old woman. I live in New Haven, Connecticut, with my 26-year-old son, Sky. I am an entrepreneur with my own business, called GotMeals. As a single mother, my time has been quite limited in all aspects of my life because my focus was on providing the best family life for my son. Developing GotMeals allowed me to worry less about serving nutritious food made from scratch. I knew I could spend more time with my son and less time cooking. I have always viewed life as a challenge made to simplify: I often repeat, "Keep it simple." The simpler, the better. I can remember playing baseball in the 1970s with all the boys in my family. I was about ten years old at the time. It was the first time I had expressed the desire to play baseball. I made a fuss about playing. When the guys were picking teams, I said,

"I'll play!"

"You can't play; you're a girl," the boys replied.

"*Dad!!!*" I quickly exclaimed,

"Let your sister play," my father commanded. I caught everyone off guard because the occasion was a joyous gathering, my father was Sicilian, that "Include your sister" remark was contrary to how he viewed females. But not me – I was different. I never knew the word "can't." I went on to grow from a 7-pound 19-inch-dark skinned girl into a super-interesting, empowered female. The old rules – "Head down, follow what you're told, don't ask questions, keep quiet" – were simply not for me.

I was a rebel born into a time in US history when second-wave feminism was on the ascendant. Gloria Steinem, leader of the feminist movement, had a gravitational pull throughout my adolescence and into my young adulthood. As a high-school girl, she appealed to my rebellion against my mother's passive role as a wife. Decorating the house, painting nail polish, and endless shopping seemed useless to my goals.

In 2007 I attended a luncheon hosted by Steinem in Greenwich, Connecticut. The times had surpassed many of the audacious statements that she once spewed about the male gender. Getting married no longer meant surrendering your maiden name and taking the last name of your husband. I led the first organized altar girls at the Catholic school church, Saint Bernadette's, in New Haven, Connecticut. The school encouraged sports, and whereas we were limited to cheerleading to the first class, it would now also include softball (aka girl's baseball).

The inner voice screamed to end Hollywood to stop the belittling portrayal of women, but my scream would go unheard by the feminist movement. Instead, it focused on women's reproductive rights. Movies, television, and magazines infiltrated the 1970s and '80s with the sitcom

Three's Company. Its leading star Suzanne Somers played a dingbat. *Hustler* and *Playboy* shoved women's twats on magazine covers and The Godfather beating the women that demanded equality. Choices were made for women by men. Women gained some leverage by a juxtaposition where the male Richard Gere, in the film *American Gigolo*, allowed women to gratify themselves in his beauty.

Media was an intoxicating social experiment created to promote norms. I finally disavowed feminism when it legitimized and even glorified prostitutes as "sex workers" going so far as to petition the United Nations to legitimize this degrading practice by desperate women to generate income by providing sex services to men. A first-time independent filmmaker named Sylvester Stallone went outside of the Hollywood system to produce a film, *Rocky*. He played a boxer depending on his wife and partner to support him on their path to glory as husband and wife laden with admiration. It was a film of inspiration lacking in the Hollywood genres of the time. The 21st century brought Game of Thrones (GoT), interchanging women heroes on the battlefield equally in the brothels. Women didn't change Hollywood; instead, sexual perversion grew. The demoralizing abuse towards women a scheme created by and for the film industry.

Producers and Supreme Court absconded America's values. The Motion Picture Code of the 1930s was overturned by the 1968 production code[1]. The equilibrium has managed to find its own norm. Standards have been erased just like the label on the jar on the cover of the book, *"I am not a gender."* A society that can no longer be offended, be it of moral, religious, or gender, must have done something correctly. The vindication is both sexes can be exploited for sexual purposes.

The feminist gave minimal effort to uplifting women to become educated and pursue careers equal to that of their male counterparts. Women have managed to tear down the Hollywood elite's veil, creating perverted scenarios to feed the minds of viewers, all while continuing to be perpetrators of pleasure paid in human degradation. In 2017 the most significant debacle of sex for play scheme came to a screeching halt. Hollywood producer/mogul Harvey Weinstein was offered up after political elites went on a

---

[1]Colbert, S. (2009). I Am America (And So Can You!). Amazon. Retrieved from: https://www.amazon.com/Am-America-So-Can-You/dp/B0047GNCVC

media rampage to impeach President Trump, based in part on a sex scandal.

Hollywood created the #MeToo movement that emboldened females to come out of the shadows to tell their stories of how they had been forced to perform sexual favors to men in exchange for advancing their careers in the entertainment industry. The witch hunt may have ended without even more indictments of famous producers and male actors when the same political maneuver was used to try to prevent a Supreme Court nominee, Brett Kavanaugh, from confirmation to the Supreme Court. More victims came toward to claim #MeToo. The test will be if honor can be restored to the workplace in a dual code that is not based on politics but liberation.

The expendable empire of pedophilia, sex trafficking, satanic rituals, and child exploitation all but revealed Hollywood's obsession with degrading societal values to achieve promiscuity for the elites to partake in pleasures of the flesh without fear of prosecution.

The philosophies and mores that we receive from society regarding education, work, culture, religious practices, and family values are called social conditioning. We are all susceptible to social conditioning. We are social animals. Social conditioning helps us create, nurture, and sustain the network of people with whom we associate. However, its deep-rooted effects play a vital role in forming our entire personality. Our perspective on life, our beliefs, interpersonal connections, and decision-making are all influenced by the people around us.

From our youngest years, when we begin associating with people outside our nuclear families, we become conditioned to seek approval and validation. Similarly, we learn that winning is one of the fastest ways to achieve acceptance and popularity in life. Being "better" than the next person – in academics, sports, economic measures, and of course, personal appearance – gets us attention, praise, relationships, jobs, and control over our lives.

We are programmed to live our lives to earn approval – and our course that extends to our appearance. We take hours to select an outfit and groom ourselves to attend a party so that no one in the room will look more attractive. We join a fitness club to get and stay in shape. And for most people, if we're honest, the motive is not to become stronger and healthier, but to achieve society's artificial standards of the *perfectly shaped body*. We work hard to improve our lifestyle and avail ourselves of conspicuous luxuries.

Our desire to look better than others and to earn society's validation sometimes turns our lives into a living hell – and the curious part about it is we don't even realize it. We even compete in relationships. We try to win over others within our sphere of influence, partners, and friends. Social media platforms like Facebook, Instagram, Snapchat, etc. understand that we live to impress others, and they help us to portray the most attractive images of ourselves to those on our "Friend" lists. We don't enjoy our VICTORY. We crave the acceptance of people in our surroundings.

Do you ever feel drained?

Do you ever feel that even after being given every blessing, do you not feel happy or fulfilled? Do you ever want to run away, leaving everything behind? The majority of us cope with feelings like these in our lives.

The main reason for that is that *we live our lives for others*. In the race to become the best and the prettiest and the richest, we ignore our true selves and shortchange who we really are. We spend most of our lives pursuing two goals: to please others and to *defeat* others. Locked in this endless struggle, we forget to love ourselves.

Consider the example of a 14-year-old boy named Charles. He was an elementary school student. He never liked studying, especially mathematics. He would always score below average grades in math. As a result, his teachers would humiliate him in front of the entire class, and his parents would scold him. It was one fine Sunday evening when Charles requested his father to sign his report card. His father was very angry when he saw his grades. He had scored only 46% marks in math, and his overall result was also unsatisfactory.

Charles's father refused to sign his report card because he was extremely disappointed. Charles told his father that his teacher would disgrace him if he didn't return the signed report card to her. But his father didn't give an ear to his plea. Adolescence is the perfect time to take ownership of yourself as Charles did by signing the report card for bad grades on his parent's behalf. When questioned in school that the signature looked forged, Charles dismissed the confrontation by owning the precarious nature of his dilemma, "My father refused to sign it," he conveyed, at which the onus was on the teacher and the parent.

I found myself in this scenario throughout my education. Eventually, life application defeats the alien concepts taught in school as we have real-life use for mathematical, foreign language, or rote historical facts. The education system is designed to introduce elements that are not tangible for students to apprehend. As a student, I was known for saying in geometry class, "I don't know when I am ever going to need to know this in life." The time came as a Realtor when listing homes that configuring land size and dimensions of structures seemed intuitive.

Learning is unique to every individual. The Russian education system assesses each child's strength in the areas of science, engineering, and the arts then places that student within a curriculum that channels the student's aptitudes to serve the needs of the state best. It may be a utilitarian concept to determine how you will serve yourself and the government at the age of four. Unemployment is not a problem; citizens lacking professional skills instead toil in the beautification of the cities, towns, and villages, be it street sweeping, scrubbing building exteriors and windows, planting flowers, road work, and making signage.

This system first envisioned 150 years ago in Karl Marx's *Das Kapital* does not reward labor with pensions or Social Security. Instead, according to the social contract, government elites control the distribution of material goods gained from labor, as private competition is abolished from the working class in favor of the greater public good.

Liberating students to seek out the best education is a fundamental right in the United States. The law provides to any student given an Individual Educational Plan (IEP) the right to a suitable learning environment. Why could Charles (in the example above) never score good marks in mathematics? The No Child Left Behind Act of 2005 provided a means for low-income students to receive academic help to close the learning gap with their counterpart students from upper-class families. Classism has become a part of a school system that separates students' needs based on income. Who cares what address you have-education should meet the individual needs of every students' learning differences? Studies showed an increase in vocabulary when students ate dinner and engaged in conversation with family members. Something as simple as eating together made a big difference in test scores compared to students who did not enjoy the benefits of family conversation. Students learn in different ways. It is time that we, as a nation, break out of the government-run public education system with its outdated curriculum and instruction methods that date back to World War II.

There is an inferior school system dividing individuals economically. WHY is the public education system robbing from children? Our public education system ought to provide equal access for students not by the ZIP code you're born into but by allowing testing similar to Russia's example that individualizes students' abilities. Why set up any child for failure in a school that is mismatched to his or her individual learning style?

When I grew up, it wasn't uncommon for students to feel shamed by the collective grading and learning protocol. Everyone is different; conforming to a one-size-fits-all education saves money for the school system, but education should not be compromised.

Elementary and secondary education provides the foundation for adult life skills and outlines at least a general vocational direction. Parents get caught up with the responsibilities of family life, homeownership, car payments, taxes, insurance, work, and challenging an outdated system that takes more money and time than individuals have. The system is rigid, lacking in the delivery to benefit all students.

Public-school employee unions pay administrators and bureaucrats obscene salaries. The superintendent of schools in my town earns $200,000 a year. School district administrators enjoy powerful union protection of their high-paying positions and job security. Have you ever heard of a lawsuit against a school official? Teachers and students are fed to the sharks as the ruling elite controls the resources with cronyism, special favors, and corruption, all in an effort to oppress and subjugate the class beneath from rising.

There are two groups of professionals that I love for their purity, teachers, and scientists. Why else would coworkers allow American history to be taught by a gym teacher or the computer teacher with a coding certificate? Teachers fulfill their requirements for teaching without regard for their coworkers to teach. All professions fulfilling licensure is good housekeeping practice and at the very least, an insurance policy that the Praxis exam hold accountability to a level of knowledge suitable for teaching. That very standard should be required for all students to advance in subject fluency, not dependent, as the current system is flawed by age and a grading system.

Waldorf and Linda Mood Bell's learning approaches are not restrictive to age and grade. The discipline is based on advancing levels earned by mastery. The concept is more humane actually, values the individual, and meets their individual learning needs. Collective learning marginalizes learning differences in favor of a primitive survival of the fittest and needs to be replaced in an effort to fulfill each individual student's success.

Redesigning an equitable education system begins with empowering the Student! Dead will be the bureaucracies that walk away, holding the money that should go directly to our children's future.

School Choice has long been follies by strong teacher unions indoctrinating student bodies to create a force of resistance. The people will eventually turn on the system that has subverted their families' ability to access any school based on merit while removing the barrier known to the privileged class as educational autonomy. Going where you want in life starts with access to any school. A school choice program empowers family's to be in control of their future and school money set up in an education bank. Taking income out of where one is educated redirects the individual to compete with skills, talent, and interest, focusing on the student's ability to achieve.

Education accounts take the birth of a child as an inheritance to posterity. Families receive $18,000 per child at the schooling age based on the income of families under $200,000. Setting students up to fail or a life of prison must stop now!

Is getting good grades really the matter to achieving one's destiny, fulfilling a life purpose? Of course, it is not, but having equal access to attend an academic institution that respects your interest, aligns with your goals ultimately will benefit students from wealthy or lower-income families the same. Anything less is oppressive. Our society is full of students and adults like Charles, who are dealing with family and societal pressure of measuring up to others' expectations. Parents and teachers become extremely indifferent when they should understand the reasons behind a child's failure. Charles had been scoring poor grades for quite a long time.

Nevertheless, neither his parents nor his teachers tried to have a conversation with him regarding his issues. They kept shaming and rebuking him, which made him feel incapable of improving. This kind of behavior from family and teachers is the main reason behind low self-esteem among kids.

Children with low self-esteem are prone to developing anxiety and stress. The constant pressure from parents and their degrading attitude elevate their stress levels to the extent that it becomes unbearable for them to handle. They can find no better way than destructive behaviors expressed as sabotage thinking until life requires some type of escape.

The escape can manifest in many toxic forms, but by having successes in life, they can suppress a maladjusted behavior. Mia Hamm's famous quote, "Success breeds success," should resonate in your head whenever you attempt an endeavor. Helen Keller is an avowed communist; however, her life demonstrates organic debilitations that can be challenged through a nurturing, supportive environment. Follow the words of teachers and coaches, and their goal is to inspire each student and athlete.

The price of success is hard work, dedication to the job at hand, and the determination that whether we win or lose, we have applied the best of ourselves to the task at hand.

-*Vince Lombardi*

As we grow from a child to an adolescent and to an adult, our beliefs grow stronger in our minds. We live the life that society expects us to live. It creates frustration because, many times, we can't fulfill these expectations. We need to learn how to restructure our relationships without people's expectations. Hollywood preys upon subtle influences that seem perfectly normal as time erodes one's sensitivity values. Knowing one's identity is ongoing and cannot be encapsulated in a fleeting moment or based on the popular pressure to be like the glamour society patronizes. My intent in writing this book is to encourage people to contemplate their essences of existence and be unique not to be rebellious or appeasing but to be pure to one's inner voice. I learned from motivational speaker Dale Carnegie in his book *How To Win Friends and Influence People*, to compartmentalize tasks. Novelist J.R.R. Tolkien wrote, "Little by little, one travels far." That was in the early 1900s. Compartmentalizing may be hard to attain with the fast-paced sensational gratification that technology offers in the contemporary realm, but greatness is achieved long-term with diligence, focus, and persevering.

We don't need to please anyone but ourselves – not in a selfish way, but in a way that allows us to capitalize on our aim in life. It is your choice to allow distractions into your life or people that drain you. I give people that complain or are releasing 6 minutes to vent. I tell them I don't allow negative vibes in my space, so I will give you 6 minutes to vent and come up with a solution. I focus on showing them complaining doesn't get anywhere; it digs a hole for you to bury yourself.

I ask throughout the regurgitation, "what is your solution" repetitively. Consider how you utilize the environment, and create the environment you can thrive in. The people we spend most of our time with have the power to mold our lives. Right from our childhood, we are conditioned to be pleasing to others. I taught my son from a young age, "You never have to give an explanation to anyone." I am not advocating blame. I am promoting a solution-based approach, aka awareness, or mindfulness. A Buddhist journey to enlightenment begins with the breath. Oddly enough, the Bible references, life begins with BREATH. Breathing is the life force; getting the technique to clear your mind will allow you to practice mindfulness.

If you feel anxious, practice breathing, and it will aid in sleep and clearing the mind. Breathe in, count to six let the airflow to your belly from your nostril inhalation, release the air gently and slowly counting to six, and repeat this process nine times. This book will serve the purpose of deconditioning your minds and making you aware that you have been conditioned since the day you were born.

We get this life only once. We should put everything in our life by our own choice. The best saying I will recite is, "A life well-lived is a life worth living." Live it Boldly. Go for what you want, and persistence is hard work. Kenny Rogers reminded us:

You have to know when to hold them, Know when to fold them Know when to walk away,

Know when to run.

There will be time to count your blessings when the dealing is done.

Expectations create an implied agreement between you and society. If you accept, people will assume you are okay with it. Learn speaking up for yourselves, or else people will keep dictating you. By not creating boundaries, you validate the agreement, and it grows into a vicarious social contract. You will most probably begin doing the same for others.

The first step to preventing people from dictating how you live is to limit your own expectations from people. No one knows yourself better than you do. No one but yourself can choose how you live and the education you receive. Choose wisely; no one will rescue you either. It is a sink or swim world. *The Verve's* song, *Bittersweet symphony* lyrics portray the road of darkness cleared by the cleansing of the mind until you can shine. You don't owe anyone, but no one owes you, success is bittersweet.

You either get bitter or you get better. It's that simple. You either take what has been dealt to you and allow it to make you a better person, or you allow it to tear you down. The choice does not belong to fate; it belongs to you.

- *John Shipp*

Chapter 2
The Choice of Lifetime

"Our lives begin to end the day we become silent about things that matter."

– Martin Luther King, Jr.

What do you do when you see a young child being bullied or ridiculed?

Do you speak up for them or choose to just walk past?

Frequently in our lives, we face such situations where our conscience nudges us to speak up, but we don't. Perhaps, we don't know how to be assertive or fearful of the possible outcomes. Regardless of the reason, when you don't speak up, you lose your chance of bringing a positive change in your society. At times people say hurtful things or pass mocking remarks to us, and in most cases, we choose to stay silent and ignore them because we don't want to land in a fight or an argument. We think staying quiet is our biggest contribution to maintaining peace in our relationships. However, that is not the case. If we don't speak up for ourselves, no one else will. If someone treats us unfairly and doesn't raise our voice against it, that would show that we are endorsing their behavior.

The following are some of the reasons that keep us from speaking up.

We are afraid of losing a friend or a relationship as a possible outcome of speaking our mind.

We are concerned about our image in the society. We think that people will laugh at us.

We feel success is proving we can do it all.

We think that even if we speak up, no one will listen to us.

We are ambiguous about our needs.

We believe that speaking up will not bring any change. Or that others know better than us.

The above-mentioned reasons are entirely based on my observation and experience. You may have different reasons not to speak up. However, most of my friends and people in my surroundings agree that they don't speak up because they want to avoid a quarrel. We choose to stay in a toxic relationship at the cost of losing our own identities. In fact, it's not about relationships only. As a matter of fact, we suppress our feelings in our professional lives as well. We hush our inner voice when our bosses humiliate us or take credit for our hard work. We want to tell them that they are wrong, but we don't. We endure this injustice because we don't want to lose our jobs. This fear propels us to zip our mouths.

I believe speaking your thoughts into reality works like a catharsis. If you keep bottling up your emotions for a long time, you develop depression and anxiety. In the marathon of keeping others happy, you become an enemy to yourself. The funny thing is, you realize it when it is too late.

Why Should You Speak Up?

Martha Boneta took a stand against the anxiety from being wronged that had built up. She had to believe in making the American value of life, liberty, and justice in her Virginia town ahead of herself. It is by giving in to corruption that we are allowing ourselves to be disenfranchised. Martha, schooled in law and opting for a pure, simple life, began farming a 65-acre farm that was met by an insidious group that spent ten years trying to remove her from her land and business. Talk about fighting city hall, that's precisely the kind of red tape that is maliciously contrived to create havoc distorting the real intentions of higher powers or the elites to destroy individuals from land acquisition.

Farming is self-sufficiency at its optimal form. Being a self-reliant in-some form can present great challenges to those in power. It may be the traditional women at the mercy of her husband's wallet, a student at the receiving end of a grading system that punishes the free thinker, or as in the hierarchy of capital familiar to systems the top protecting competition and closing anyone posing a threat.

Martha's Liberty Farm is the story of speaking up, believing in the right to be heard, and insidious communism that wages war on individual rights in an effort to abscond state power for the control of resources for the perfidious few[2]. I am convinced the inconvenience is a burden that silences many from being courageous or resourceful as never to keep quiet. Until gross aggression is brought to light, it

---

[2]Catherine, M. (2019). Martha Boneta's Stand for Liberty. The Epoch Times. Retrieved from: https://www.theepochtimes.com/martha-bonetas-stand-for-liberty_2995523.html

can only be defeated by causing Helter-Skelter to attract others. Awaken others to bring injustices that you have first-hand knowledge of not as an agitator but as a sympathizer to rid the wrong for future generations. Expose corruption brought to your doorstep to gain power for the individual. The powerful ruling class uses subtle means to destroy each one that remains silent and then some.

Believe me, if I could "shut up," I may have had an easier life. It is to the chagrin of many that I am still talking. It is only natural that I would share my thoughts out loud. My Dad always referenced me as an open book. I like to think authentic. It is bizarre that being transparent seems to mess with people.

Does that grab you the wrong way?

Let me say it again; being authentic is in opposition to freedom. How much is the world allowing women to be independent, self-evolving to serve themselves as a whole?

I give more than needed, especially when unsolicited. People try to intimidate one into silence by using their power – any form of suppression results in blackmail. Aggressive or passive rejection takes on the shape of gossip or exclusion, mainly aimed to subvert dialogue. Well throw me out, insult me and talk about me... I will not shut up!

I believe speaking up is necessary because it releases your stress. I wonder how people can sleep at night with so much in their hearts and minds. We all want to say something in almost every situation. Oftentimes, we have to stay silent even when the entire situation keeps replaying in our heads repeatedly. In such situations, we wish we had an option to handle it differently. These thoughts eat us from the inside out. I find "head down, follow what you are told, don't ask questions, and keep quiet," was not for me any longer.

I rebelled against the injustices that remained unconquered at a time in the United States that did not represent the entire country. The idiosyncratic House of Representatives stood as a reminder that powerful women were needed to change the male-dominated landscape for females, especially inserting powerful women into the legislature. Theoretically, women and children were seen and not heard of. Professional women that can work and have a successful family differed in the environment I grew up in compared to the powerful female the future promised for educated women.

Times were a-changing a women's traditional identity to end the secretary careers or homemakers that long served men. The expression that influenced my endeavors from an all-girls' college preparatory high school imprinted a message of "behind every great man is a strong woman." To me, that meant no man was any better than me. In fact, they needed women to function. Presently, society has placed women as pursuing careers with all the old responsibilities of homemakers or giving up procreations.

Regardless of lifestyle, the future is here, and women didn't do anything wrong if they decide to have a family and pursue a career. Equal for both men and women are the life change the moment a child is conceived. Mommy's and Daddy's, whether same-sex or heterosexual sharing responsibilities of child-rearing requires speaking up and facing resolve for balance. Contributing to change means staying silent will inhibit the potential you can harness collaboratively.

We need to understand that people do not mind readers. They won't know what you feel until and unless you make them aware of it. Let's take the example of a girl, Tisha. She was an African but lived in the USA. Obviously, her English accent was different from all her American friends in school.

Tisha's friends always mocked her because of her accent. She felt bad but never expressed her disapproval. Her silence made her friends believe that she was fine with all that humiliation. As time passed, Tisha stopped participating in all of the class discussions and debates. She had developed a mindset that if she spoke up, people would laugh at her. It shattered her confidence to the extent that she became a major depression patient. If Tisha had initially given a shut-up call to her friends, her situation would have been entirely different today.

The scenario illustrates that people will always find a way to ridicule you if you allow them the room to do it. It's YOU who has to stand up for yourself. I am not asking you to get into a fight with people when you disagree with them. There is always a respectful and courteous way to show others where the boundaries are. You might not observe it, but when you choose to speak your thoughts out, you inspire others to follow your way. People begin seeing you as their mentor. Speaking up makes you a leader. In friendships, marriage, and in work settings, the structure of human interaction represents a micro-dynamic, applied in a macro system as an entrepreneur the ability to understand negotiating with others demands a presence or a seat at the table. A macro system is found in church auxiliaries, boards of companies, community committees, and governments.

Failure to represent a majority is met with frustration. Let's look at another micro dysfunction similar to Tisha's peer confrontation previously discussed. Presented is an example of a child's family relationship impacted by their parents, the husband, and wife scenario. If the talent of negotiating is not mastered early in life, it repeatedly appears until the chain and ball are broken from causing a debilitating hurt.

Let's visit Elisha's life, an adolescent entering his teenage years and Tyron and Alexandra, a husband and wife. Both have family structures with happiness dependent on expressing one's feelings and being met with a reciprocal validation. That validation is respect! Elisha is unable to manage the routines of school, getting on the bus, eating a healthy breakfast, and taking a snack and water canteen for after school sports. His uniform is not cleaned for the sports game after school; he didn't complete the homework assignment that is due needless to say he feels unprepared for the day ahead. Similarly, Tyron tells Alexandra he has a meeting out of town. Alexandra already left with navigating the family's equilibrium feels dumped on. She can never count on planning because of the unpredictability of everyone in her family schedule.

One of two scenarios can happen in a fight or negotiation. A successful scenario begins with "Respect," of which Alexandra must keep the blame out of her mouth. She can rattle off to Tyron a diatribe of troubles and how his priorities or lack of interest affect the family and her. She can scold the children for their lack of priorities, but it adds wood to an already burning fire.

Once the mastery of negotiating through RESPECT is practiced, it will be automatic and help eliminate chaos in life. Make a choice: do you want to live with emotional insecurities, loneliness, peer pressure, illness, poor school performance, loss of faith, divorce? When we feel ignored, neglected, criticized, or make anyone else feel inadequate, we perpetuate the destruction that belongs to blame, shame, and disrespect. Listening to the overarching interpersonal theme each other is presenting is step 1.) Ask yourself, what is the overarching pattern the problem presents? For Tyron, he has a lot of activities, and being prepared the night before will give him the success he should have to begin each day. Stated with empathy and not condemnation or blame, Tyron, you have a lot on your plate, do you think you can eliminate one or two things so you can get to everything fairly? No one needs to help Tyron pick up the pieces; it is his problem to manage. Many family dynamics rely on one person fixing another person's problem, which ultimately leads to the individual unable to learn valuable skills to navigate throughout life.

It also dumps on the person who always pitch hits everyone else problems. The person stepping in to rescue everyone will feel like a doormat and lash out, causing a house of cards to collapse within. The person that is the fixer is disguising the lack of respect for themselves by absorbing others' problems. If you are the "fixer" always running to everyone else's rescue ask yourself,

"How does it serve me?"

Let's take a moment and think of practicing four steps to any mutual compromise 1.) Recognizing what pattern Tyron is presenting? Would it be fair for Alexandra to deal with her husband's absence and feel dumped on? Where is the respect he should have for himself, for his wife and family obligations? If she attacks him, a fight will erupt because if we learn anything from interpersonal relationships, 2.) it is that we do not "Blame" as long as you have respect for others that will lift the direction to the higher ground of mutual empowerment.

That is what love does; 3.) it builds up; it does not tear down. What causes us to attack are old ways of behaving out of feelings of frustration. 4.) Practice your new scenarios for at least three years. It is easy to master a life lesson; practice substitute the new habits quickly and replace the old patterns – it is worth your happiness.

Alexandra has learned to reply to her husband by saying, Let's look at our schedule. It sounds like the meeting was last minute, is this the Baker project you have been working on. Engagement shows I see you; we can figure something suitable together. Tyron is presented getting dumped at work and then bringing it home and transferring it to his wife. She has to be successful in her own career if she is all things to everyone, she will feel disrespected, unloved, and undervalued. It takes time to listen and receive the words the other person is communicating, but you must use their words in a conversation to verify you understand the pattern.

Alexandra asks you to have an unexpected meeting? You must have had to shuffle your work schedule around to accommodate the meeting. That is what Tyron threw at her, she heard him. Mutual respect sees the other person. Alexandra and Tyron head to the kitchen for breakfast; it is there that they check the family schedule each morning. Apparently, Tyron will have to make alternate plans; they both have a scheduled commitment tonight is back to school night for their children.

Alexandra negotiated with Tyron. I will take the children out to eat before "back to school night," but tomorrow night is your night for dinner. She adds Tyron dinner plans for the following evening to the family schedule. When we are young, developing intrapersonal behaviors modeled by our parents or sometimes we have to learn ourselves by trial and error. These skills establish early work ethics. Knowing the formula that has been mimicked for you by two working parents becomes your ethic by osmosis. To allow fair competition in a work environment town hall community agency, universities and provide role models known as

"Mentors" support to broaden career possibilities to those children who otherwise begin with a disadvantaged paradigm.

Insurance to support marginalized youth, specifically growing up in a one-family home, provides resources to change the trajectory of a lacking work environment. A parent quickly realizes the relevance of socializing a child to successful outcomes is something that you have been taught the regiment of skills will benefit equitable access throughout life interpersonally.

I painted my own world gained by the confidence I was given from having a stay-at-home Mother who taught Nature and a Capitalist Father that cherished his family. My college years were filled with living on the edge. I did whatever I could do. The opportunities were endless. I grew up with my grandmother, Lucy. I think it was there that I learned a woman is as brilliant as she will allow her talents to be applied. My grandmother lived a simple life; she was an example of conserving resources and setting boundaries that others respected. She lived in a family of eight men. Her father and brothers owned a grocery store. However, my grandmother's father realized that she was more efficient than all her brothers when it came to running the business. She could do all the calculations in her mind at the grocery check-out. He decided that she should take care of that grocery store, but my grandmother wanted to be a nurse. She chose her way and handed over the business to her brothers. When she got married, my grandfather died quite young. My grandmother didn't remarry and brought up her children on her own. She lived her life the way she wanted, not having accountability to anyone, living by herself seemed easy. I spent a college year domiciled at her residence.

Living with her gave me a sense of female empowerment, and the ability to measure the damage conforming to expectations can cause. To negate an individual's purpose for the good of the family, my Grandma sacrificed her dreams of becoming a nurse. The daily newspaper and local news constructed her paradigm. The alphabet news anchor Walter Cronkite ended each broadcast with "and that the way it is," reporters were not questioned; the stain of reporting had influences of social control. Molded in a time that limited the individual mind to become a part of the culture jeopardized her authentic contributions. Forgoing a business and relying on elites in the media allowed policymakers to be the stakeholders as if they were clairvoyantly filled with predilections to impose prejudices on the masses. Realities became vicariously distributed to society by the media movie stars.

I have not forgotten to think of news anchors as nothing more than entertainment. Ratings are what pays, not authenticity. It is vital to sack off the paradigm imposed upon us by allowing a limited worldview to impose a pseudo account filled with ideology as one's existence. I witnessed an entire generation relying on TV, be it news, sitcoms, or idealizing movie stars in a contrived environment relinquished the first-hand experience to create their own constructs – good riddance to the days of propaganda.

Presently, the age arrived compelling, diverse interaction to experience, which should allow the dismantling of limiting thought that leads to barriers. Integrating experiences with social influencers can be sinusoidal at times. However, living your life the way you want consciously, purposefully, requires instinct and the ability to make good judgments. I got into politics after I tried hairdressing – a funny story my Dad's mother gave my plans of owning my own salon, the Kibosh.

While attending cosmetology school, I explained what I was doing; her reply was very frank. No one in our family will wash and cut other people's hair. In reflection, my feminist stances began with the influence of the women in my family. I am the biggest supporter of women's empowerment. However, I have observed that these days, people perceive feminism quite differently. I have seen many women supporting abortion as a part of their freedom. It is certainly not true.

I want to convey a message that there is a big difference between being a feminist and being selfish. Aborting an unborn innocent soul is not freedom nor means to women empowerment. Owning power is advancing the responsibility of nurturing a child strategically. A master of women's power is decisive, asking critical questions and weighing her options before consequences that can create a disadvantage. It is keeping power that allows you to capitalize on "no plan is a bad plan" it is better to plan a method of contraception before engaging in fortification or not giving up your power. If you think having a child will limit your academic endeavors or career perspectives it may be worth holding off plans to have a baby and to wait until later in life to fool around rather than to be tortured with the absences of your unborn soul, your baby's life and your emotional health are worth designing a plan. Every life is worth saving young or old unless we behave like Hitler.

Women can live a life according to their own choice along with their children as well. Life is a gift, and abortion is at its lowest point since 1973[3]. If both husband and wife choose to work in order to improve their lifestyle, they can look for ways that can support them in nurturing their children. Your elderly parents can be a big help. Moreover, you always have the option of hiring a nanny. When you are determined to do something, the universe opens the gates for you. I opened a Nanny agency in 1995 called Care Bears. I used a logo of the most caring bear Winnie the Pooh. Winnie the Pooh is the Zen we all need to be like. He represents perfection because, rather than having all the answers, he is at peace with the law of attraction. Faith in humankind is regenerative; by having faith in others, our faith in ourselves is replenished.

---

[3]Stanglin, D. (2019). US abortion rate is at its lowest, but restrictive laws aren't the likely cause, study says. USA Today. Retrieved from: https://www.usatoday.com/story/news/nation/2019/09/18/number-of-abortions-us-drops-guttmacher-institute-study/2362316001/

The cycle of life is seen in his whimsical confrontation with the natural progression of life. A symbiosis is sustained as a juxtaposition to scheduling and family planning. Life is about the nuances "The detail is in the small stuff." My dad cited a verse from the Old Testament. "A wise man built his house on rock the rains came in the house stood strong. The poor man built his house on sand, and when the rains came, it was destroyed" – Matthew 7:24.

Whether we build it on our faith in God, as the verse suggests to follow God's law of obedience is to *rely* on God. Today the future steps in that would be the rain; if we create a generation of resilience, the rock is faith in ourselves and mankind, making good choices and strategically creating goals that allow us to contribute to the planet. It would be remiss not to discuss balance in life; harmony creates a framework of equilibrium.

The classics warn mankind against the forces of pleasure. Preserving goodness is designed to provide a supportive environment based on purity. You can't get morality from relativism, nor can a hostile practice bring liberation. Profound good emanates from the respect of life. It is self-determination, as seen in Dante's "The Inferno," preserving ourselves is found in resisting detriments that demoralize us. Watching a hateful newscast, listening to harmful lyrics, associating with negative people infiltrate our core and before long deterioration sets in robbing us of joy and leaving us in darkness. Guard what the eyes and ears see and hear so to as the heart follows (Matthew 13:15).

A law established by our forefather's sets in motion unless a person poses a threat to society, the individual is not a threat. The law believes in you to make good judgments. The architects of society did not see men as masochists. The evolution of the planet improves as minds think in more advanced design, a push to new modalities increase progress. Einstein theory of quantum physics along with Astrophysicist agree a vibrational force allows for a trajectory within a universe propelling humankind to a transcendentalism.

Choosing to foster positive skills to enhance ourselves begins with listening and seeing others. Strength within families advances with communication to develop the skills most needed for faith in others established through practicing respect begins with the love "you" establish for yourself. Parenthood should always be a planned decision.

Learning how to make educated and calculated decisions include strategic planning and begins with a schedule. Like collaboration used in relationships, as in businesses understanding each other, opens doors to put in place structures for cohesiveness. Apart from learning to live on our own, we also need to learn how to make effective decisions that affect the planet.

Certain things in our lives can't be undone once it's done. If we harm others such as an unborn life, we cannot get to the common good propelling all to aspire to what is a legacy of support. In the book The Shack, the nature of freedom is presented as a duality.

"Questions are freedoms doing what you want to do, or the intrusion of your souls' sickness be that inhibits and binds you, or the social influences around you or the habits that have created synaptic bonds in pathways in your brain. And then there's advertising, propaganda in paradise. Inside that confluence of multifaceted inhibitors[4]."

---

[4]Young, WP (2012). The Shack. Retrieved from:
https://www.goodreads.com/author/quotes/15481463.William_Paul_Young?page=3

Chapter 3
Discernment is Judgment

Traditional values can bring order and ward off anxiety caused by the uncertainty of the unknown. Developing discipline allows patterns to be accessed and categorized more coherently to allow the greatest capital. Making advancements begins by assessing the facts (gathering information), and creating solutions.

The turkey story exemplifies why challenging previous ways of doing things are an evolution to progress. It's often been said you can't expect to get somewhere different if you keep riding the same horse. We are creatures of familiarity. To be a trailblazer is to think for yourself, take calculated risks, go for self-discovery, and break the mold.

The Turkey Story

It was a Thanksgiving, and all the family members were gathered together the women were in the kitchen sharing in the preparation of the turkey they were seasoning it and basting it and ready to put it into a pan then in the oven when suddenly the turkey did not fit into the oven. They turned it to the left and the right, they took the turkey out of the oven and back in, and nothing would work. They could not fit this big turkey in the oven. Now, what would they do? Thanksgiving would be ruined. One of the guests recommended removing the wire racks, but that did not work either. Someone remarked to change the pan.

The host told how the significance of the turkey meal was to use her great old grandmother's pan that ever since she was a child honored the family tradition of cooking the Thanksgiving dinner. If you change the pan, maybe the turkey will fit in the oven offered her guest. She replied, "my great grandmother, my grandmother and my mother all cooked the turkey this way, I followed the family recipe, I don't understand why turkey will not fit in the oven," she concurred, "the oven must be too small. Perhaps I need a bigger oven?"

Her niece came, grabbed a pan, scooped up turkey, and switched it to another pan she opened the oven slide out the wire rack and placed the turkey in the oven!

Einstein's cliché of the definition of insanity describes repeating the same actions repeatedly and expecting different results. My son shared with me a book from his fourth-grade summer required reading at Green Farms Elementary school in Westport, Connecticut. It held deep within its pages a lesson of finding your path that isn't always on the path everyone else follows.

"The City of Ember" Jeanne DuPraur defines a group that lives below the ground, never exploring beyond what they have been told lies above their societies' territorial limits. Above are the lights, endless food, and an entire world they have never allowed themselves to experience. They have grown accustomed to what is below some in the group are discontent and out of necessity sacrifice the known for the unknown.

The edicts of following can restrict growth without growth; we are at the whims of others. The only thing you can regret is not taking every opportunity to make your life authentic. It is your experience – go experience. The days of sticking one's head in the sand are over. It comes down to a question of trust. In order to trust, a judgment must be weighed. Presented with factual evidence, we all will arrive at the same conclusion. Serious life choices have an inherent value to individual meaning. Meaning or value that individuals hold does separate man. Below are life choices

To pursue education

To rent or to own

To work at a high paying job or a job we love

To buy a new car or lease a car

To live where you grew up or to move away

To keep friends who gossip or to end friendships

To marry who?

To have children, how many

To send children to public or private school

To stay home and raise children to continue to work

To take care of elderly parents or to provide care of a nursing home

To buy life insurance

To eat healthy to take medications

These questions and life choices are distinctly different than what color I should paint my house, studying botany or nutrition, biking to work or driving, eating dessert or not. There are some choices, while individualistic in nature that ultimately reaches a certain result, there are no guarantees.

The probability is more likely that by keeping your choices in a circumference that targets life goals, the chances are increased that you will live the life you have worked to enjoy.

What is your paradigm? The following narrative should infiltrate your thoughts when deciphering to pursue a choice. Are you a skeptic based on evidence or trapped in the dictates' confines that others have laid upon you? Two men were in a prison cell with a window. One prisoner asked the other prisoner, what do you see when you look out the window? One prisoner saw the prison bars while the other saw the beautiful field.

Conditioning can play a part in how we see our futures, but it is our responsibility to guard our thoughts and the influences that shape thought. As far back as Hippocrates long before Jesus, nonetheless, a teacher like Jesus, he helped shape the understanding of human temperaments? Our organic disposition qualities are innate in how we are programmed that do not need to be changed but do need be respected if we are to be at peace with how we function best. The four characteristics that were developed hold true 1,500 years later, people are people we don't have to live out of fear if we understand what makes us tick.

1.) Phlegmatic

They are okay with the status quo, easy-going, and probably not going to speak up.

2.) Choleric

Boss type, direct to the point, opinionated, persistent, hot-headed and stubborn, impatient, and will make themselves heard.

3.) Sanguine

Lovers of beauty, lacking task commitment, extroverted, social, loud, careless, enjoys the pleasures of life.

4.) Melancholic

Analytical, self-conscious, enjoy solitude, shy, sensitive, self-reliant, and moody[5].

The personality that we are born with like clay can be molded to become a masterpiece. It is in an enriching

---

[5]Bennett, A & Bennett, L. (2012). The Temperament God Gave Your Kids: Motivate, Discipline, and Love Your Children. OUR SUNDAY VISITOR.

environment that we learn to thrive. And as you can tell from the above, if someone with a Sanguine personality has all of the newest materialistic objects, it would make them aware that beauty was superficial. How do we challenge ourselves if we are comfortable with no challenge?

Life will inadvertently change, and being able to transition may take a longer time for a melancholic individual, but the train will return to the station and voila you are on the train and adapting instead of resisting change. If we want to be strong, we begin by strengthening our weaknesses. You have heard nothing is free. It takes a big investment in allowing ourselves to be open and to be vulnerable to take risks that will have no guarantees and make us feel uncomfortable. There comes the point when doing things, and we may not even care that it doesn't seem worth it to us to get involved. What if you felt no one cared? When I got involved in my first political campaign, I wanted everyone to care as much as I did about politics.

It was the 1980's everyone was working and making a lot of money it seemed they were too preoccupied to care. Complacency is the time the enemy strikes. Like a banquet set or a king feasting on gustatory delights, his opposition gains strength to catch him off guard and attack to destroy the distracted king. The first political campaign I worked on was for a Connecticut congress candidate, Bruce Morrison.

When tasked with developing a campaign contributor appreciation event, I did. I named the event "Politics can be Fun" to attract more people to get involved. Present-day society has awoken, and the fun is as if citizens cannot be pleasured by good times rather play a part no longer by laying down their lives in battle but seeking out the fun stuff, and it ain't free, and it no longer is as fun as it once was.

Brainwashing! Free is the operative word pandering to influence what otherwise should be objective research – using media propaganda to tie the United States' hands behind its back while other countries advance! Socialism relies upon shaping a false worldview with nothing else than films as a tool used by closed countries lead by dictators. Political documentary or objective reporting intentionally designed to push an agenda to influence their base. Shaping thought, fear-mongering, creating constant threats, and uniting with vigilance a call to duty.

Search on the Internet North Korea's propaganda. A film created by Kim John masterfully to lead his community to protect themselves from the evil empire, America. The United States is thematically portrayed as eating the birds from the trees in the dire cold to keep from starvation. China signed an agreement to allow Google to provide the internet to the world's largest population with one condition. Google agreed to create a barrier to world information in favor of State-controlled propaganda. Are you familiar with the old saying if your friend talks about other people in your company, then you can only predict that such a person would talk about you in your absence? The inference is that if Google is controlling the medium in other countries, it is Google's modus of operation. I am not paranoid, but the FCC (Federal Communication Commission) exists to protect us from an Orwellian Government imposing a loss of the individual's privacy. Agreeing to be controlled allows one to be an active participant in making the choice of Big Government enterprise –

To choose or not to choose? Some years ago, while helping my son researched a macro-economic assignment taken over the summer at Gateway Community College in New Haven, experts from a journal or newspaper were presented, which showed, "Green House effect" was brought about by the government trying to control the oil drilling internationally. Intern, the largest oil company, produced research to vindicate its business.

Years had witnessed every changing name from "Global warming," and its cause is today's "Climate change" and a whole new range of contributing factors. However, for the past 12 years, I would search for the article that I read for my son's research only to find a consensus that the world was going to explode unless we stop consuming products. With all refutation removed from the debate, one had no alternative to deciding what to believe in an educated manner. Instead, the elites controlling the messaging would feed us a version of the ramifications the American society and not the individual was having on the destruction of the planet.

Recycling is beneficial. An altruistic program would rely on reusing, recycling, and compostable as a successful model. Instead, a Hollywood scam benefiting the elite bureaucracy while fraudulently preying on the weak by agitating the mob and compromising school children is erected to produce a debilitating future and hamper the United States advancements in favor of a global regime.

The world regimes would all have to participate in consciously reducing waste that could contribute to an overall increase in colder weather. Weather, by its very nature, is always changing. Here in Connecticut, there is a saying, "if you don't like the weather wait ten minutes," I still cannot figure out what happened to the dinosaurs? Did the United States cause the extinction of the Velociraptor? The 5th century BC paleontologist studied organisms' evolution in the environment chronological data simply does not support an environmental disaster from overconsumption of products[6]. However, I endorse the futility individuals could perpetuate by becoming less wasteful and repurposing plastic food containers, using cloth towels while banning paper towels and fining households for throwing food away rather than making composite to replenish the earth of vital nutrients.

The weather has been changing from the beginning of time. That is what the weather does! Allowing the government to solve the problem specifically denies individual responsibility in favor of giving up freedoms to change societal behavior with oppressive laws, taxes, and a

---

[6]SIRI knowledge (2019). The scientific study of prehistoric life

set of rules that impose more government control over citizens.

A DenTek floss pick used to remove teeth tartar would do more to solve disposable waste than eliminating a plastic straw. However, the genius government's "token" resolution to plastic waste insulted common sense with a plastic straw ban.

An embarrassment to resolve the long list of far larger intrusive 2.5billion disposable coffee cups in the UK yearly[7]. Businesses will do a far better job than relying on the government to implement behavioral changes. Take, for instance, Starbucks reusable coffee cups, or oceans, and rivers "clean up" teams by the charity Common Seas. The greatest contributor of waste is not being addressed Sandra Laville, sheds light on 14,000 tons of microfibers culprits from clothes and tire.

She and Jo Royal from Common Seas report recommend banning paper towels, wet wipes, imposing taxes, and

---

[7]Smithers, R. (2019). Gatwick hosts the UK's first airport reusable coffee cup trial. The Guardian. Retrieved from:
https://www.theguardian.com/environment/2019/jun/10/gatwick-hosts-uks-first-airport-reusable-coffee-cup-trial-starbucks

eliminating fishing tackle, tire dust, and microbeads[8]. The government will never go against long-standing relationships with excessive, indulgent, violators. Groups of concerned communities are at the forefront to raise awareness and stop using disposable products. Individuals amassed to support "Project aware" to solve the cleanup in Deerfield Beach, Florida June 15, 2019, collecting 3,200 pounds of plastic. Marisa Spyker reported in the publication *Coastal Living*, 633 Divers just set a world record for collecting ocean trash off of Deerfield Beach on the east coast of Florida. Think before you "use" where will this end up? Before you overuse shower and beach towels adding to unnecessary laundry surge and long-lasting effects of detergent released into the water.

Humans can reduce the environmental infiltration of the water for a cleaner earth. Reuse, conserve, and eliminate waste. I do not believe in climate change but advocate for recycling programs. Weather is continually changing, and the elements are eroding with time. I am the first one to

[8]Oakes, K. (2019). The search for a cleaner, greener plastic. The Guardian. Retrieved from: https://www.theguardian.com/environment/2019/jul/07/the-search-for-a-cleaner-greener-plastic-ocean-pollution-landfill-bioplastic-pla-composting

propose an alternative to fossil fuel, but common sense seems to have been overshadowed by a confluence of brainwashing to shape a paradigm shift.

The pioneer of more government control on corporations, businesses, and individuals giving away their freedom is all thanks to Al Gore. The man whose wealth orbited to billions selling gullible sympathizers a narrative that the world is exploding. The invisible dictators use their influencers to tell us how to live as they fly off in their rewarded personal airplanes, which is the number one contributor to harmful emissions to our planet. Profiting off of making society aware that conservation has an impact on waste begins with an individual's behaviors; instead, the rich get more power, more wealth adding more regulations on the little guy.

Consuming a disposable product is for the consumer to control their buying habits, but that will not change until the public stops lining up for Dunkin Donuts, McDonald's, and Starbucks. The responsibility to conserve starts inside each home. Freedom and the liberty to choose are being bullied by a dominating class and marginalizing divergent approaches to solve garbage waste, environmental preservation, and sustainability. Comparatively, when untold deaths are the cataclysm result of infanticide, disease, drug epidemic, poverty, and garbage waste.

The power grab is using climate change as the better noir to rouse emotion and instill fear for the silent few to play us like puppets. Sincerely, follow the trail of who paid for global warming now climate change altered "research," manipulated "science." Intellectual, political honesty looks at both sides; free information without controlled internet searches. Again, taking care of our environment begins at home, i.e., plant a garden, use eggshells, banana peels, coffee/tea grounds, for composite, when taking out foods bring home food containers, avoid pickup takeout restaurants/hotels using plastics, Styrofoam or establishments that are not recycling and above all recycle garbage

I was a BirthRight Volunteer. Part of addressing abstinence began with reaching teens. What better place to reach teens than middle school and high school. The Superintendent of schools in my municipality denied the BirthRight presentation to address students. The students receive condoms but are not allowed to hear a presentation on pregnancy choices. The Birthright message was being blocked while Planned Parenthood's message was being endorsed. That type of cherry-picking infuriated me because all students should be given as many tools to make an informed decision. Especially the greatest decision we will ever make: giving away one's virginity as an act of love or experimenting out of curiosity? In a civil society, the implication of sex resulting in pregnancy and the choice to give life or end the life of an unborn child require a conversation, not a band-aide. School officials resisting the alternative to dominate and cause hardship seemed primitive, yet the remark, "sex is an animalistic instinct," they're going to have sex anyway lacked empathy as to the unforeseen repercussions students were intentionally ill-equipped by design. Prophylactics abortions and child sex schemes are big businesses that the powerful political interest that needed to protect children would sabotage the pay to play backroom deals.

The schools have become a breeding ground for using a public school for left-wing indoctrination, aka PROPAGANDA is an outrage. The message "You only live once" is offensive to censor a message; the party of death gives you a free pass to play! A young woman will live with regret all the days of her life, directed by the sinister schemes that control the messaging perpetuating a distorted reality instead of a reasonable alternative message. Silencing life and voices that present another option is bullying. The powers in control have been allowed to gatekeep. The result is being witnessed in the destruction of the civilized family and economic planning. It seems if another message should be presented, people may choose in contrast to the desired elite prescribed beliefs.

Therefore, all outside ideas must be prevented from talking about the current one size fits all distorted realty. Imagine if, at a community school, an abstinence program in favor of the Right to Life was offered! It has never happened, nor will a Pro-Life group ever be allowed to speak. America is losing our freedoms, and it is happening in the classroom. The Uganda model was used in Africa to stop the epidemic of AIDS occurring from sexual promiscuity. I visited Uganda's centers set up under the George Bush administration to promote abstinence reducing 90% morbidity[9]. It saved lives from sexually transmittable

[9]Allen, M. (2010). War on AIDS Hangs in Balance as US Curbs Help for Africa. Wall Street Journal. Retrieved from:

diseases allowing women to pursue an education and become independent. Unless divergent perspectives are presented to include all members of a society fully, individuals become forced by the influence of dissemination and subversion of ideas resulting in groupthink. Witnessed in groupthink is the loss of individuality in fear or intimidation. One conforms rather than face peer alienation or mocking. A homogeneous view should be something all Americans speak out against. The solution for more government ("the nanny state") to solve personal responsibility is the problem.

If smoking cigarettes is attributable to cancer, why the push to legalize marijuana? If unprotected sex leads to pregnancy, why engage in recreational sex? If spending more money than one makes leads to bankruptcy, then why do banks issue unrestricted credit cards? If schools exist to educate, why is there a determined curriculum? If eating unhealthy leads to obesity, then why health care. The push for more government rest on the idea that someone determines what is good for others. The elites gather

https://www.wsj.com/articles/SB10001424052748703906204575027442437944112

resources that the plebeians gave up to their superiors. How do a husband and wife work together, or should the husband exploit his wife? Should anyone be given the power over anyone? Who decides, You do! The freedom to choose requires personal responsibility, not coercion.

Do you agree that while some rule and some follow that society has to have a majority representation and the dissenters are marginalized? The existence of a demonic group bent on power was apparent in 1905 and active in Eastern Europe until the Nuremberg Trials. Crimes against humanity repudiated Communism. President Regan, 1984 may have provided infamous "Tear down this wall," a visual antidote that implied Communism had been destroyed.

Europe may have confronted the promises of Socialism, which ultimately reward the few leaving a slave state communism promised. Relinquishing resources, i.e., land, work, education, health care, transportation, procreation, and food supply, abandons self-determination at the behest of the greater few. Tactics are present within the naive, unsuspecting country that is kept isolated from identifying the postulates put forth in the tenants to undermine and cause influence. Palestine, Ukraine, Lebanon, Poland (Samuel

Farber, "War is a Racket," Jacobin, Lessons from the Bund, 01/03/2017) are familiar with the oppression of political parties and suppression of individuals who advanced Capitalism and God.

America is a young country cutoff from exploring the history of political regimes in existence with a vengeance to dominate. Thrust upon us are the forces of one government and controlled elections. People in a free election celebrates the vote of the people, not a rigged system. The proletariat blurs the lines of which side is getting cheated by voter suppression. Protests are expensive, staged, and uses voters as pawns.

The diabolical network will accuse the just of corruption to deflect their disinformation as a tactic knows as espionage to infiltrate mob unrest. It is intentional that social justice, slogans, and creating the "in" crowd to deliver absolute power to the elite while leaving "out" and creating rage against diverse thought. Do American citizens want to be forced against their will to work for a Socialist system that usurps power from the ingenuity, liberty, and bloodshed of our Great War heroes and citizens for the hidden enemy that forces adherence using mind control.

The United States generally abides by an individual's right to self-determination. What causes harm to oneself is only a concern if it causes harm to others (Eric Tennen, Is the Constitution in Harm's way? Substantive Due Process and Criminal Law pdf. www.scholarship.law.berkeley.edu, pg 1.of 37,). Marry a woman abuser, gestate unwanted babies, become obese, uneducated, unhealthy, unsanitary, drug dependent, gamble and bankrupt the price to pay is to the pied piper. Is it true that these problems are exclusive to the individuals' bad choices in life? Should these proclivities be a shared cost to society? The larger government becomes, the weaker the individual grows.

The individual no longer is liable for bad consequences; the citizens take care of the slackers in a "Nanny State." Providing a common-sense approach requires accountability to address debilitating social ills, not an endless amount of taxpayers' money the proverbial "safety net." The comparison if a parent fixed the calamity caused by a wayward, disobedient, young adult, the parent would be regarded as enabling bad behavior. Parents resolve a "tough love" approach; no action requires the parents to respect bad choices, but it is the individual's choice to self-correct.

Governments are creating policies for the individual to produce the greatest good for parents who provide the house's rules and reward success. The saying comes to mind, "I love you, but not your actions."

Republicans say people are rich — and poor — because of their own efforts; Democrats more likely to point to a person's circumstances and advantages

In your opinion, which generally has more to do with ...

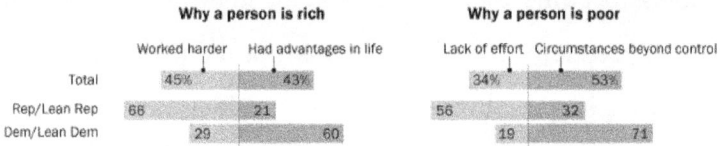

	Why a person is rich		Why a person is poor	
	Worked harder	Had advantages in life	Lack of effort	Circumstances beyond control
Total	45%	43%	34%	53%
Rep/Lean Rep	68	21	56	32
Dem/Lean Dem	29	60	19	71

Note: Don't know responses not shown.
Source: Surveys conducted Nov. 30-Dec. 5, 2016 and April 5-11, 2017.
PEW RESEARCH CENTER

When is a good time to provide unwanted assistance? Is the status quo acceptable relative to how much pain the individual can endure before surrendering to a majority norm before they kill themselves? Risk mitigation is a practice in business that maximizes a return and increases opportunities in developing proactive measures that would otherwise fail. Suicides are increasing among young adults by nearly 30 percent since 1999, according to the Center for Disease Control and Prevention (CDC). Disease is likened to the ravishes of wars that rob our society's young males.

The policies of the Big Daddy Government seek to erode self-identity replaced with the mob mentality of declaring war on the family, and it's once venerated weekly obligation to attend mass (What happened to letting "boys be boys?" Prager U September 15, 2019, for fellowship, biblical guidance, and belonging to a higher standard enriched by love, support, and kindness.

The protest to the Vietnam War in 1960's and early 1970's lead to volunteer military services. It is not hard to distinguish an average society and what makes an exceptional society. Take, for instance, the Israel Defense Service Law requirement. Despite gender from the age of 18, the service in the Israeli Defense Forces is mandatory (but not compulsory) (The Jewish Agency for Israel, Army ages and Laws, 03/2016 archieve.jewsishagency.org) instilled with discipline, civic duty, honor in serving something bigger than themselves. Taking away the right to pray and serve one's country has had a tumultuous impact on the youth for generations that ensued. The journey of self-existence provides every individual to seek out protection and the space to grow with dignity. Learning to be able to defend themselves, be of service to others and accountable are the proclamations of identity for which is absent in the United States Michael Reichert, "How to raise a boy" (4/9/2019, Tarcher Perigee) defines while girls emotional intelligence is designed to accept love, boys are not reciprocal inclined. The male can only trust their environment and loved one with the "trust test." In a time when society has replaced family connections, male role models, peer pressure to be sexual, and attack hyper-masculinity, boys struggle to find direction in their lives and security to trust their identity. All too often misunderstood and unable to develop the tools to contribute to something bigger than themselves.

Chapter 4
Silent Influencers

Since my college years in the 1980s, I have been obsessed with politics. The mixture of talking too much and political resolve always caused consternation among conversations. I probably spent most of my life objecting to socialism. I felt capitalism taught a work ethic. I believed in providing the greatest amount of freedom; one should work hard. It seemed logical that work begets wealth. It followed that wealth allowed for more freedom.

The freedom to go to better schools, travel when you felt you needed a vacation, and order anything on the menu. No one talks about the downside, the relentless years working through the night, a mind preoccupied with a constant entanglement of thoughts. I was doing all the physical work for many years with little social life and mostly alone – the financial burden with equipment, insurance, and taxes in my own business is a big responsibility. No one minds providing paychecks to the laborers. The main reason to start a business is to provide jobs. The risk of never knowing if a capital return would follow one's endeavor is not for everyone. The years would witness the great debate that I spent ½ my lifetime in classroom studying and in later years observing in practice. I would hyper evaluate which best served the whole of society the haves or the have-nots.

The solutions to consider that are timeless are: 1.) Redistribution of wealth or 2.) A contribution from a work ethic that produces wealth. Redistribution means that some people want more out of life and are fortunate privileged to have the skills talents and yes intelligence to achieve more than others. Believing that redistribution comes in and takes from those that have made achievements and distribute their good fortune that fell from the sky to others who had greater difficulties in achieving monetary success.

I want to point out that while struggles to advance one's wealth may be the result of bad habits, i.e., overspending, etc., redistribution of wealth cannot change the course of bad habits. It only can give to what is believed to be equity for an intentional suppression of those that have more of the wealth. While living in an affluent community, I learned a metaphor of a grading system, ironically, from a grade school child, Emily. A decade later, onto graduate college while staying active politically. Her awareness between equity would beg the question; Does giving "money" to any segment of our society ensure monetary equality. Fill in the blank if you're a Socialist in the case scenario exchange "grades" for "money" Below is the grading system employed by academic institutions that purport distribution of resources:

There was a classroom of 12 students, and the professor came every day diligently and took attendance called out the student's name everyone attended his class the assignments were handed out, and the students performed. He enjoyed teaching, and the students enjoyed learning. One of the students complained he didn't agree with the professor's grade at the end of the year. The professor questions the student that is a grade that you received for the semester. The student protested, but you gave everyone else higher grades, and you gave me a failing grade.

The professor explained the students attended every class they participated and turned in all the assignments. You did not hand in the assignments you did not participate in the class discussions based on the required readings, and you had infrequently attended the class. But I took the final exam? You showed up the last day and took the exam and received a "D." The professor questions the student did you think you didn't need to attend as the others did, and you should get the same grade as they did. The student explained I am in college. It's no big deal that I missed class. Your class was too early for me to attend. I party at night and sleep late. College is a lot of fun. The professor reasoned the nights you were out partying your classmates were doing their work; they made sleeping adjustments to sleep earlier the night prior to making it to class on time, and they learned the material asked of them. The student took a classmate that received A's over to the teacher pleading you could give me some of her "A," and we could both get "C's."

The professor answered, but she worked for her grade.

The time to allow individuals to manifest their reality in a century that has witnessed economic wealth cannot be blamed for leaving anyone out. Still, the individuals' choices are the culprit. It is not up to society to tell people what time to go to sleep to wake up and be most productive. Living horizontally raises everyone with the ability to act upon self-actualization. Since the culture I was raised in highly coveted food, I was paralyzed to encounter people that place no value on what they eat, never plant a garden, or have empty refrigerators but manage to offer a drink of beer. Having different values makes you work hard to provide for yourself or not to provide and rely on day to day whims.

Old Version

The ant works hard in the withering heat all summer long, building his house and laying supplies for the winter. The grasshopper thinks he is a fool and laughs and dances and plays the summer away. Come winter; the ant is warm and well-fed. The grasshopper has no food or shelter, so he dies out in the cold.

> > MORAL OF THE STORY: Be responsible for yourself! > >

Modern Version

The ant works hard in the withering heat all summer long, building his house and laying up supplies for the winter. The grasshopper thinks he is a fool and laughs and dances and plays the summer away. Come winter; the shivering grasshopper calls a press conference and demands to know why the ant should be allowed to be warm and well-fed, while others are starving and cold. BBC, NPR, MSNBC, CNN, and New York Times show up to provide pictures of the shivering grasshopper next to a video of the ant in his comfortable home with a table filled with food. America is stunned by the sharp contrast.

How can this be, that in a country of such wealth, this poor grasshopper is allowed to suffer so? Pikachu appears on the View with the grasshopper, and everybody cries when they sing, "It's Not Easy Being Green." Mylie Cyrus stages a demonstration in front of the aunt's house where the news stations film the group singing, "We Shall Overcome." Bernie Sanders exclaim in an interview with Anderson Cooper that the ant has gotten rich off the back of the grasshopper, and both call for an immediate tax hike on the ant to make him pay his fair share.

Finally, the EEOC drafts the "Economic Equity and Anti Grasshopper Act, "retroactive to the beginning of the summer. The ant is fined for failing to hire a proportionate number of green bugs and, having nothing left to pay his retroactive taxes, and the government confiscates his home. Hillary gets her old law firm to represent the grasshopper in a defamation suit against the ant, and the case is tried in the

9th circuit court. The ant loses the case. The story ends as we see the grasshopper finishing up the last bits of the ant's food while the government house he is in, which just happens to be the ant's old house, crumbles around him because he doesn't maintain it.

The ant has disappeared in the snow. The grasshopper is found dead in a drug-related incident, and the house, now abandoned, is taken over by a gang of spiders who terrorize the once peaceful neighborhood. > > MORAL OF THE STORY: Work is not a bad four-letter word Private innovation differs from the public systems of development and research. The irreducible characteristics cannot be excluded because the investment that puts "skin in the game" controls the thirst to achieve a clearer direct focus.

The public elements rely on collaborative work efforts directed by red tape and timelines seen in a private setting as luxuries undermine the grit behind America's success. It is comparing China to America rather than the lagging economic factors of most state-owned businesses. China competes by copying the innovations produced in a free market economy. Taking away an incentive to create an individual's destiny relies on controlling wealth acquisition.

There is little ambiguity in a society that does not allow reciprocal wealth to be matched with work; the individual's plot in life cannot be changed. Human toil is interchangeable with output diminishing the pursuit of the individual's purpose.

Private innovation occurs in an austere work environment. It is set forth from self-determination, persistence, resilience, and trust indistinguishable forces that project the lone star striving for excellence for the public good and not primarily for a collective reward in the form of a paycheck and job security. Public bureaucracy limits potential in favor of security. Production is artificial because the individual has no challenges to compete. Innovation is compromised for lower standards, and ultimately masking pride in one's work deteriorates initiative.

Waste wants not. Did you ever notice the value someone has towards something they earned? I saw this in college with a window left open in the middle of winter. I asked the student to my chagrin; the window was open because the heat was up to high. Evidently, the school didn't have separate thermostats. That is bad practice, sloppy and poor communication allows for an easy solution to go unmanaged. Throughout my travels, every window that is open in winter irks the environmentalist in me. It is the best way to cure "it's not my problem," or "there is nothing I can do about it," to charge violators into creating better solutions. I guess the ones it would hurt least is the ones with nothing to lose or those who could afford to pay. The people in the middle always bear the burden for the rest of society.

There is no money in cures. Conserving energy, practicing alternatives to medical visits, and not using disposables may be the solution to less is more. In 2016, the alternative medicine industry reported an estimated 14.3 billion dollars. Increasing sentiment to live alternately has impacted living off the grid and replacing plastic bottles with canteens. Awareness can be the force of change.

Dr. Pinsky practices a holistic approach to health and exposed that many of his patients are no longer living because he was directed by the board of medical physicians to rate pain with each patient, documenting a rating scale from one to ten for each patient to indicate their threshold, and prescribe addicting pain pills for those indicating four or higher. That Big Pharma push increased revenues in 2016 to over 200 billion dollars. It doesn't seem like the Government had the people's best interest when taking control of health care, creating drug dependency to the tune of 4.5 billion prescriptions (Center for Disease Control and Prevention). The COVID- 19 witnessed the same kind of medical steering, giving doctor's specific instructions death certificates attributed to COVID-19 received $13,000 reimbursement from Medicare insurance. Death certificates with medical treatment receiving ventilators from COVID-19 brought in $39,000 for hospital billing (www.factcheck.com, retrieved 5/13/2020).

It is no surprise looking at the way The Department of Motor Vehicle, Amtrak, or the buses function that any entity that wants to implement an imperialistic allocation of resources is dipping the pot, they're invested at your expense. Recently, at a visit to Motor Vehicle, I estimated form the line ticker that if there are three lines and each process 600 motorists at a medium fee of $100.00. The Motor Vehicle would rake in $180,000 a day! That explains why it is not privatized. One location makes a quarter of a million dollars. If each state has 50 locations, that state is collection 9 million weekly. No motorist should have to stand in line yet alone pay additional taxes. Motorists should be greeted with card readers as they drive up for services. Further incentives to give the motorist discounts toward state tax obligations, purchasing of cars, maintenance, and car-sharing programs would show that the states that advocate "sharing" would do better at it themselves. The saying that for every seat there is an ass would suggest we are asses believing the Government is going to take care of us.

The course is clear with the replacement of people in the work sector by Artificial intelligence; many people will rely on paid unemployment. Can we think far enough into the future of jobs and see a time not too far away from where families can enjoy quality housing in quality transportation, eating quality convenience food attending to school and work from home and participating in spa services as recreation activities. Vocations will be obsolete, but a new crop of professions will meet the new society with an infinity for family enjoyment.

Mothers will no longer be in search of child care; there will be no absent parents or latch key youth; we are approaching a positive child-rearing unit. Self-contained homes will need less space, efficiently designed to provide state of the art conveniences for all. The very wealthy can afford to distance themselves from plebeian society, maybe inhabiting a planet or two. The hidden resource holders control the assets; the rest of the people can fight among themselves in an endless circle. Michael Bloomberg, "Mr. China," controls the media message in two world powers The US and China. His conglomerate media empire tentacles range from radio, television, magazine, finance data, digital technology leading the world in a multimedia platform.

His power to wield the direction of the wind is not a force of nature but the sheer magnitude of resource capital. His breadth spans 130 countries, 80 million consumers, 20,000 employees, 167 offices (bloomberg.com, Bloomberg Media Distribution). Powerful to join forces with the global communist party and sell Americans a story of redistribution of wealth. The message is disseminated by a hierarchy of players creating mass compliance to obscure the true intention to dominate assets. In a Capitalist environment, waging war with the greedy few who dominate control is a continual competition to balance power for the many. Economic prosperity is fairly attained when government and powerful monopolies are prevented from controlling business, therefore, allowing all citizens equally to have a part of the dream. Grant.gov awards entrepreneurs by fostering innovation and the opportunity to compete for a stake in the game. An advanced protocol has been put in place that allows regular citizens to apply for capital to start any business. The guidelines provide targeted mandates to ensure compliance for the commercialization industry standards. The Corporate model, combined with the government, is Capitalism. It would ensure that government waste is held accountable while offsetting state power to any individual meeting the Government grants oversight measures.

The balance between rewarding individuals and giving them the ability to succeed in a business generates productivity, advancement, and innovation, not to mention wealth! In 2016, $230,672,881 in wasted taxpayers' dollars on items like getting Zebrafish addicted to nicotine or a self-cleaning toilet and bringing Serbian cheese up to international standards[10]. Is there a feeling of who we can trust to dispense the resources justly? Do not be easily convinced that the government is the power broker if left to

---

[10]Sen. Paul. (2019). The Waste Report. Retrieved from:
https://www.theepochtimes.com/sen-paul-says-officials-wasted-over-230-million-in-funding-as-debt-grows_3164597.html

its own volition. Which group will you trust to dole out equitable sources? Do elected officials represent the collective group better than the built-in company mechanism, aka "the bottom line approach," or the biased media, the academics, the brand makers, influencers, i.e... Hollywood? Would power make them unjust? Should we rely on the current application allowing the individual to earn his plot in life? How do we guarantee civil liberties to protect the vulnerable from being exploited by the wealthy who use lawyers to take from those that can't compete or lack representation?

Chapter 5
Eroding Parties

It's not really that I hate capitalism; I really couldn't care less what kind of system of economic distribution we have, as long as it works for the good of all.

— *Oscar Auliq-Ice*

In America, the names of political parties and political movements don't always reflect what they actually stand for. It may be confusing to be affiliated with a party in name while it's platform is so much more than what the party represents in the name. It may be associated to reflect values it does not actually practice.

The voter may be told the popular propaganda from changing party principles. If you're a capitalist, you vote because you believe that work is a right. However, the US doesn't have only one group claiming to represent itself as a "labor party." In the United States, a faltering two-party system limits ideas by using party labels and ideological campaigns designed to agitate voters to vote for one party or another.

Top Contributors, 2017-2018

Contributor	Amount
American Federation of Teachers	$3,823,552
National Education Assn	$2,013,880

Contributions to:
Democrats ■
Republicans ■
Liberal Groups ■
Conservative Groups ■

While labor and public-employee unions notoriously donate 98% of their political contributions to the Democratic National Committee (DNC)[11]. Dues-paying union members aren't given a choice of which candidates for office their "contributions" support.

Unions disguise the voice of the average American, which pales in clout to the special interests' muscle. People are getting railroaded by the Democratic machine's ideological influence — the party spends $1.1 billion of members' dues without their knowledge or approval[12]. The Democrats hold 70 % of the wealth in the United States. That

---

[11]Melchior, J. (2015). Dues for Democrats. National Review. Retrieved from: https://www.nationalreview.com/2015/11/unions-spend-dues-liberally/
[12]Barone, M. (2017). Which Party Is the Party of the 1 Percent? Capital Research Center. Retrieved from: https://capitalresearch.org/article/party-one-percent/

is why progressive is out, and populism is in. The voters in a united effort are pulling together to liberate themselves from the invisible destructive forces embedded in government as the unelected leakers, opposition forces, and resistance. Elections are selling a popular brand while absconding power that cannot be used as a platform the people would vote on. The enemy disguises the issues as a covert operation to derail fundamental rights without being forthright. I knew a man that frequented stripe clubs, wined, and dined the girls; he was their sugar daddy. I asked, "why do you use these innocent women for sex," his reply, "I know who they are, and they know who I am." A reciprocal agreement rather than an illusion is illustrated best by a poem called the snake;

On her way to work one morning

Down the path alongside the lake

A tender-hearted woman saw a poor half-frozen snake

His pretty colored skin had been all frosted with the dew

"Poor thing," she cried, "I'll take you in, and I'll take care of

you"

"Take me in tender woman

Take me in, for heaven's sake

Take me in, tender woman," sighed the snake

She wrapped him up all cozy in a comforter of silk

And laid him by her fireside with some honey and some

milk

She hurried home from work that night and soon as she

arrived

She found that pretty snake she'd taken to had been

revived

"Take me in, tender woman

Take me in, for heaven's sake

Take me in, tender woman," sighed the snake

She clutched him to her bosom, "You're so beautiful," she

cried

"But if I hadn't brought you in by now you might have

died"

She stroked his pretty skin again and kissed and held him

tight

Instead of saying thanks, the snake gave her a vicious bite

"Take me in, tender woman

Take me in, for heaven's sake

Take me in, tender woman," sighed the snake

"I saved you," cried the woman

"And you've bitten me, but why?

You know your bite is poisonous and now I'm going to die"

"Oh shut up, silly woman," said the reptile with a grin

"You knew damn well I was a snake before you took me in

"Take me in, tender woman

Take me in, for heaven's sake

Take me in, tender woman," sighed the snake

Oscar Brown Jr[13].

The Democratic Party has long ceased being the party of
"labor"; the Washington Republican Party that is
marginalized and painted as indifferent, or has the false
narrative deceived our eyes? The Republicans consist of
what is referred to as the heartland of the country. In contrast,
"the Deep State" based in unelected and unaccountable
representatives and resources remain allusive. Pandering to
the utilitarian worker, that inevitably live paycheck to
paycheck, contrasted into a class of the haves and the have-
nots of ideological differences.

The economic and political elites concentrated in New
York, California, Seattle, Boston, and Chicago are dictating
to the rest of the country an imbalance of power leading
Americans into a class war. A day without the triple As –
alcohol, air-conditioning, and Apple gadgets – would be
unbearable for an ideology that controls the spending. These
elites preach by a guilty conscience for their comforts, waste,
and spoils as they throw crumbs at the proletariats (us) to tax
ourselves to death. It is an uncomfortable irony that many of

---

[13]Genius. (2020). The Snake. Website. Retrieved from:
https://genius.com/Al-wilson-the-snake-lyrics

the political elites live in communities – San Francisco, Chicago, Manhattan – with the greatest wealth inequality.

The solution – raising taxes beyond what middle-class residents of those communities can bear – is the opposite than one would imagine. Many mayors of these cities promote a progressive "liberal" approach that allows the poor to live on the street in their own excrement while laws are enacted to protect the "uncivilized" from the "civilized." A proposal to erect affordable housing in a time when "off the grid movement" reckons with forcing that group to once again live on the grid. Inherent in street life culture are two groups 1.) the mentally ill/addicted, 2.) the dropouts corporate or system freeloaders – free from paying The Man. It is counterproductive to say to an entire group of people that have given up on the rat race that you must continue to be a rat-like us.

Some people don't want to deal with the pressures of paying a mortgage, taxes, electric bills, child support, lawsuits, etc... Exasperating the human code of civility by public officials not allowing police to enforce loitering, public disturbance, drug use, panhandling only to add to the homeless encampments. Don't separate yourself from your brother feeling superior by job title, beauty, social milieu; all citizens will rely on each other or destroy each other.

What has been forgotten is that in times of hardships, United States citizens historically pull together for one another. The people will be vastly different that we will be called to help and or rely on for survival in the future or on a planet holocaust. The Christians have been known historically as the originators of charity. One of the ways religious organizations help individuals are spiritual. Another way is to support students from low-income families to attend schools that prepare them for college and invest in their future. Providing scholarships to access education that otherwise would not be offered to everyone has lifted thousands out of generational poverty. The edicts of the faith a student master is to "give back." The Church has faced friction with governments as far back as the beginning of time. The biblical (Matthew Ch. 22, v. 15-22) reference Jesus reminds us to "Give to Caesar what is Caesar's, and to God what is God's." This means to continue faith-based charity and not coerced taxation to meet the marginalized among us.

The state has suppressed or outlawed organized religion in Communist countries. Some of the most inspiring architecture is found in churches. Society cherished the clergy that saw families through hardships. Our contemporaries would be hard-pressed to find donations to build the grand cathedrals of the past. Increasingly inherent biases have emptied church pews anticipating God removed from the hearts and mind bowing to a political system. The Democratic Party has become the proxy of the Church, built on the tenants of charity. Tithing 10% a tax instituted by Jesus as a Christian obligation to serve others. Faith-based solidarity is conveniently masked too supplant the end of religion. Limited resources from the faithful are subject to less and less to give as the government imposes high taxes that might otherwise allow citizens to choose a faith-based initiative of their choice.

Secular rites of worship have replaced and silenced programs that do acts of kindness in the name of religion. The all-powerful elite has taken over most faith-based operations redistribute works of charity as their own. All the while collecting tax money and religious donations, bleeding the disingenuous programs fraught with an agenda of replacement. The days of Christians contributing works of public charity – schools, hospitals, orphanages, food pantries – have been replaced by state-run services (e.g., food kitchens) that help make marginalized communities more dependent on the Technocracy who hold the reins of state power. The prerogative progressive party has highjacked a two-party election. Politicians are vying for the demise of America, selling us out to lobbyists, Political Action Committees (PAC), and phantom elites in a ubiquitous charade geared to cause chaos.

How long will we allow fighting amongst ourselves while the harm to weaken families, individuals, and social mobility is lost? Parties have morphed into a regressive tyrannical ruling elite, a cabal with allegiance to global power transferring manufacturing to untraceable foreign police states and forsaking the common man (The Next Revolution with Steve Hilton 5/17/20 | Fox News May 17, 2020, youtu.be/bPg4yY4e2gQ). The unelected Deep State is subverting policy, law, and surreptitiously marginalizing communities, a power grab to destroy a flailing religious people and bow to the one-world government is at large. There are two types of Christians: the politically savvy and the apolitical. The goal of both is to lift people up, they muscle up, side by side, doing the community work alongside their fellow man. Parochial schools may be on a path to extinction, but the hearts of many believers through fellowship are unavoidable.

Everyone can pick which lifestyle advances their need. Maslow illustrates man's needs are basic, we are all the same, but our survival mechanisms differentiate us from one another. At the end of the day, it is the value that man honors that affects his reasoning. The values one aligns with causes them to meet their need, respectively. Charity fills a void for self-reliance in times of hardship; reliance on government entitlements creates a generation of dependence, as seen in the past 80 years since the New Deal was established.

Individuals can make their own way in life by habits of hard work that should in itself generate security. These people are referred to as individualists. They are the fabric of the world. Hurt they bleed, knocked down, they get back up. There is an independent mind that does not organize with others, but recognize the best in humankind is to choose for themselves. Mavericks that self-sustain, unlike the controlled mob. The individual that identifies with a group offers another kind of sense of security, inclusion, by social cues, belonging by peer review. Belonging to others through loyalty occurs. What has been taught in school, they follow. They vigorously challenge outside schools of thought that go against teachings. They are in favor of the collective good; the state is in charge of doling out resources to meet human needs.

Resources are subjugated for the few to powerful for the common man to demand independence from. The good of society can best be met for the good of others through a system, a bureaucracy. The bureaucracy has all the power to determine what is good for the many forsaking the individual. An individual left to their own devices is full of self-interest and greed. Therefore, it is required only to allow an individual to give up that which is unnecessary for survival to the state in the form of taxation.

Taxation ensures that all can be taken care of by the collective good of the State. If you're a Marxist-Leninist, "the State" is the solution to resolve the disparity of individuals without questioning personal choice. In a perfect world, the people are self-determining, freely producing without s coercion of social guilt. Emotional fear is used to condemn good and distort beliefs. Them vs. us creates division. It intentionally demonizes others and uses the gullible individual to do the bidding unsuspecting social design to create an institutionalized force to deliver power to the elite brokers the Politburo politicians, bureaucrats, USCC federal, state and local public school, journalist, religion, Hollywood sitcoms, films, media conglomerates organized as a disinformation mechanism. They are designed to suppress thought and speech. Your ingrained thoughts become programmed. Immune to the political forces at play, a transition occurs within society, causing unrest, maybe even anger toward dissenters.

Milton Freedman's example of Capitalism is Man exploits Man and views Socialism as the polar opposite. The paradox is free markets create greed, but for who? The alternative taking what others in the free market earned, is that greed? Let's name it for the collective good. Leo Tolstoy was invited to see Capitalism in America. He was taken to a city and, while walking in a neighborhood, noticed children were playing as a limousine drove past. The boys stood back in awe. One exclaimed, "I am going to have a car like that when I grow up." Tolstoy said, "In my country, the boys would have picked up a rock and thrown it at the car," that is the difference between capitalist and socialist. The dream is limitless, not limited. Removing barriers not imposing obstacles is equality for all at its very best offered for those who want it. Why the foreman does not make the same salary as the philanthropist, s/he would not come to work, s/he would no longer benefit the collective good of the production. Outsides/ he may save h/er/is wealth, become an entrepreneur h/er/ himself, but innovation, the self-propensity is not found in a distribution State. The greatest harm occurs when hope is exploited for a belief that ownership is unachievable.

There is always a person that doesn't want to work. Nineteen million capable, able workers choose structural unemployment (Bingham, Michael, Manufacturing, New Haven Biz, October 25, 2019). Job creation converts the disengagement, contrast that with a system that provides an incentive not to work, one that pays nonworkers to collect state programs or utilize litigation as an economic activity to fight the system for what they feel they are owed. Mutually disruptive to happiness, fulfillment, and progress. Relying on the government makes individuals feel invisible. The

19th century achieved the greatest wealth and, with its wealthy donors. Wealthy people are charitable. There are only so many fingers to put rings on, only so many cars you can drive, or houses you can visit. Giving is an attribute that should be rewarded. Public parks, Private colleges, Museums, theaters, boys and girls' clubs, and soup kitchens all exist because of philanthropists. Mark Cuban, Alex Rodriguez, Tony Robbins, etc., are examples of lifting up, inspiring, and creating opportunities. Money gets stuck at the top in big Government. How we champion new ideas to provide a trickling of money to advance human ingenuity begins with investing in people. The solutions that support individuals will provide equality for all.

The tax code for billionaires encourages foundations to provide life education, transportation, vocational training, and developing skills to overcome impediments freeing up the individual so they can advance. Government is not the solution to make the difference in people's lives, but entrepreneurs that have experience with the climb to success are the models to cure the disparities. It then moves the government avarice of self-seeking corruption, preventing money from traveling upward instead of monies reinvested in individuals to reward achievements without directly burdening the struggling masses. Communities ensure fortifying the individuals that produce a collective asset. By changing one, all are made better. The government's responsibility is to protect its citizens from gangs, violence, drugs, insidious forces, institutionalized system collective bargaining, climate change, racism, classism, health care, illegal immigration, used to dissolution society, and prevent equality. Members of the government must be required to live by the laws they impose.

Getting back to work after sheltering in place to avoid the COVID -19 plague spread has given authority to the state government to enforce policies that have an economic stranglehold on free enterprise. The government remains impervious to create laws that restrict the income of citizens without the income of the legislatures themselves being affected. Sanctioning laws for citizens should be done with the same adherence by politicians. When the politicians' paychecks stop is the only time representation will be equal. The organized voices are loud and influential over those that are unorganized. There are over 26 registered Communist parties currently in the United States (www.political

partylist.com) The labor, Freedom, reform, solidarity, international, revolutionaries, progressive, social, and workers parties. The names are interchangeable with socialism. These political parties are fast at work and aggressively seeking to alter the minds of citizens. Replacing ingenuity with resistance tears down equality.

The diversity of ideas begins with delivering power to the people, not management from wealthy bureaucrats emboldened to advance a party to power to represent the common man. The Whig Party or the Federalist represented by Hamilton opposed the Democratic-Republican Party. The original Republican Party of George Washington Abraham Lincoln and Thomas Jefferson, previously called the Democratic-Republican Party, enhanced freedoms for all enthusiastically fighting for sovereignty from England, the emancipation of slave's and gave women the right to vote (suffragette movement).

Similar to the times in modern-day 20th-century politics, parties are changing what they once stood for. The Whigs wanted a united front of allegiance to England reigning supremacy over the individual, a bigger power impenetrable to accountability. Liken to 2020, the fight between

Capitalism, the individual is given the power to rise above government intervention and the Liberal approach of a bigger powerful government to distribute resources. Epic times are encountering a political transformation. I believe the common people want their power back, free from government exploits. The once young country has grown up reflecting on historical evidence that too much government is oppressive.

The anger between parties fueled a revolution. The backlash from the mob that beats down the force of change has been long at work – complacency fuels disenchantment forging a schism between the workers and power brokers. The tax burden agitates the people to upraise weaponized with disenfranchisement, slowly demanding the party that dismantles the system.

The Democratic-Republican Party no longer exists. The name once meant that the people since 1789 elect the president because the Federalist party of 1816 ruled by intolerance, suffocating common people by taxation. Political loyalty to one party requires careful study. Deception relies on believing, following, and adhering to one party. The opposition that morphs to overthrow a two-party system becomes a tyranny. The diversification of parties has become challenged. Clearly, a one-party system under the guise of different names is deceiving the voters. Sticking together as a badge of ingrained honor for inclusion fills a temporary void, and feeling a part of something bigger for the greater good the damage is, it removes your defenses. Trusting what the party represents can cause one to give away rights until, finally, those at the top run off with the resources.

Question all groups that demonize another group. When you hear yourself say "they" referring to a group unlike yourself, you are compromised, programmed, and serving an agenda. To deprogram, ask yourself am I being coerced by a set of false values, how can I rely upon that these values are self-evident. Learn the other side; all sides engage outside knowledge from older countries, older constitutional history, other paradigms – be different.

Corporations employ workers; in addition, it pays 93% (Scott, Hodge, Tax Foundation, US Business pay remit 93% on all taxes collected in America,5/2/19) of all the taxes collected.

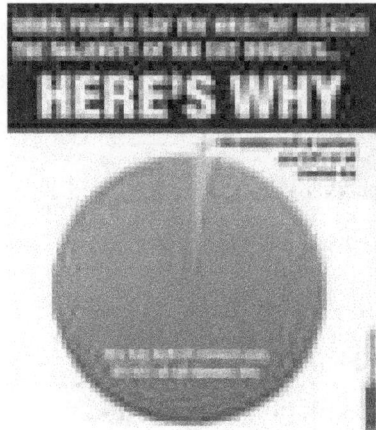

Be careful you don't bite the hand that feeds you. Tax the Hollywood billionaires off-shore bank accounts used to launder their money, including the politicians who take bribes from lobbyists. Trillions of dollars brought back to our country from off-shore accounts should support our citizens' monetary accounts. These accounts can improve lives simultaneously, providing tax-free benefits (website, sheet-offshore-corporate-tax-loopholes/, retrieved 5/15/2020.) We can't take care of immigrants when we have problems accounting for money inside the US, burdening US citizens for unfair wages of immigrants in their country of origin can be allocated by a global standard of wages. The off-shore accounts can be used by altruistic entrepreneurs providing a humanitarian effort for equality. The damage of undocumented people cause is a confluence of an off the record monetary exchange contributing to nefarious greed. If we allow them to be unaccounted for how as an advanced society, are we any better than the counties they're fleeing from. Get them documented; it is the honorable thing to do. The Civic group is being sold a bill of hostility towards themselves. Pushing communal identity has alienated man from man. Disenfranchised from the wealth they are weaponized to tar and feather "the man" why work for making someone else profits, the worker complains, "I do all the work, the owners are fools," "I will stick it to them" such a mentality is invisible classism.

The worker agrees to increase taxes and complains that "the Man" is cheating them? What is passed through to the worker is lost hope. The ruling elite keeps the social favors flowing with approval, acceptance by a false sense of social security, belonging to "The Group." Groupthink builds on disastrous results. Silenced are the dissenters, intimidated from free speech, alienated from belonging is the collective punishment to non-conformists. Inclusion is sold out by the media who pitch hit for their friends' financial interest at the cocktail party you will never be invited to attend (Avlon,

John, The Military-Industrial Complex is Real, And it's Bigger Than Ever, 7/11/2017, thedailybeast.com). The social beast desires to be a part of the group. The illustrious invitation imposes on all who play are greed, corruption, and a blind eye to the biases of pay to play schemes. In jeopardy are transparency, impartial reporting, and diversity of thought. You're not practicing acceptance by hanging out with pundits or the divergent ear piercing, tattoo informal occasional drug, sex, and rock and rollers as long as you hear what you want. Political parties should run on their record, not hide behind superficial bully pulpits.

Gone will be the days when the party posies a candidate based on their ability to raise millions of dollars from campaign donors. An insidious decay is perverting the opportunity to resist the perils of diversity. Dictators run a party that tells its base which to vote for. Limited government that allows charities to optimize humanitarian services removes the lure a political party can use to gander votes. The charitable tithing uniquely empowers the individual while maintaining accountability. You may think you are a highly evolved generation, and your forefathers could be erased that it has all been done before. Then take a look at Seneca, a figure who pondered thought, trained in philosophy, an advisor to Niro in the 54 BC, a believer in organized behavior resulting from resilience, and divine purpose practiced living a peaceful life.

"For it is dangerous to attach one's self to the crowd in front, and so long as each one of us is more willing to trust another that to judge for himself, we never show any judgment in the matter of living, but always a blind trust, and a mistake that has been passed on from hand to hand finally involves us and works our destruction. It is the example of other people that is our undoing; let us merely separate ourselves from the crowd, and we shall be made whole. But as it is, the populace, defending its own iniquity, pits itself against reason. And so we see the same thing happening that happens at the elections, where, when the fickle breeze of popular favor has shifted, the very same persons who chose the praetors to wonder that those praetors were chosen."

To take away the corporation in a fit of envy without realizing it in its place is another ruler of the goods. The Bible warned us when the Levites demanded G_d give them a ruler. How many times in the Old Testament did G_d encounter Mans ranting requests? The tribes were warned to secure their independence from other cultures, procreation (not to mix races), and remain sovereign. The people turned their backs to obedience and entered confusion, dependence, and downfall.

Saul was the first appointed ruler. Skeptical that God would be present in daily affairs, the Israelites chose to be ruled rather than trust the consecrated word, community compromises, and self-determination. Similar to the Slave state as G-d warned against, but societies develop a sense of security by becoming followers, giving away power opens the door of oppression. In the US, the top fortune 500 companies are regulated by a Code of conduct referent as Corporate Responsibility. Every business has governance for ethical behaviors with a bottom-line goal to ensure the public good of shareholders.

Companies seem to be the object of disdain among the government elite bureaucracies, in which no one can be held accountable, and the State dictates to the masses. American's can live by the rules of history rule or be ruled. The Taliban in 2011 brought down the Twin Towers, killing thousands before their attack on America ended. It was hard to punish the Taliban because of its elusive nature. The Taliban was not affiliated with a government. It was not responsible for imposing sanctions. It could not be prosecuted because, in essence, there was no particular entity to negotiate with. The power brokers control all the world's money as seen by the Taliban as the powerful elite that pulls strings, creating chaos, but is invisible to reproach. A company is much more visible and is not going to risk the hardship caused by indiscretion. Why not use corporations' success to benefit from? The creators of wealth enrich us contrast that with the politicians that live off of that wealth. We can do better!

Freedom is never more than one generation away from extinction. We didn't pass it to our children in the bloodstream. It must be fought for, protected, and handed on for them to do the same, or one day we will spend our sunset years telling our children and our children's children what it was once like in the United States were men were free.

–Ronald Reagan

Chapter 6
Baby Got Back

*"People call me a feminist whenever I express statements
that distinguish me from a doormat."*

– Rebecca West

Gender equality is a basic human right, but when it comes to access to opportunities and decision-making power for women and men, our society faces a persistent gap. Typically, oppressed groups get pulled into "equality" by becoming more like the oppressor rather than the oppressor group becoming more like the oppressed, i.e., it is acceptable in society for women to wear pants, but not for men to wear dresses.

While Joan of Arc makes a noble effort to be a gender-neutral pronoun, the vernacular use of the word "human" is in need of an overhaul. Erase the distinction between male/female in the effort to be autonomous for the sake of gender ambiguity. People can just be that which they are rather than investing so much thought as to what they are not.

We usually don't know the biological sex of animals other than humans when we see them passing or reading about them in the news. So, there's no choice but to write s/he or just pick one randomly if we are insisting on gendered pronouns. I think that is a major reason why we have relegated other animals to "it." Joan Dunayer suggests that if we do not know the animal's sex, we can just randomly pick "he" or "she," but linguistically, there's still a dilemma created by the binary.

Guaranteeing women's rights and giving them opportunities to reach their maximum potential is critical not only for acquiring gender equality but also for meeting a broad range of international development goals. Empowered women and girls contribute to the health and productivity of their families, communities, and countries, creating a ripple effect that benefits everyone.

The standard of seeing the color of a person's skin, size, shape, all contribute to preconceptions. The title of the book highlights the biases that exist for people that do not conform. This is about recognizing the erudite presences that condemn a belief outside of one's own. It is hard to question your own paradigm. How can one begin to challenge the scholarly teaching meant to program learners? It is by learners replacing labels coexisting without creating animosity for any group. Seeing beauty in all allows everyone to be uplifted without an agenda.

Black is white, and white is black. This view of nonproliferation can do little but embrace without an ulterior purpose. It does mean being a non-conformist is closer to becoming a purest if it is authentic. How do you get to the point of undoing all the propaganda that has the power to condition thoughts and reactions to our environment?

We may be unaware it is happening in every yoga class. In every Christian teaching "love your brother/sister (neighbor) as yourself" The antithetical truth that some arbitrators can be appointed to do what is best for all is causing incredible discomfort as society is confronted with a new age philosophy. The inception began with Pokémon. Soon after the cards, the games, and movies of Pokémon, a truce to determine fairness was added as child's play "rock, paper, scissors (RPS) (www.nature.com)" dating back to Chinese culture.

Realized behavioral outcomes or predictability goes out the window. All have the same chance to win based on fate.

Imagine an unbiased society free from the pressure to influence outcomes. All players can potentially dominate in a whimsical chance of fate. The opportunity to dominate is a mixed strategy.

It seems the Emperor of China had an equitable model to determine decisions without advantaging one or another. The millennials are the group using a strategy built on randomness. The worldview of millennials is being shaped socially, emotionally, culturally, educationally, politically, and economically. How does one feel in control? Here is the point at which causes the environment to collide with a personal view. One can sit back and leave life in the hands of chance or deliberately move to impact chances of success.

This is an age-old enlightenment question. Self-actualization is a struggle. The Hindu faith believes that by mastering kindness to others and serving God, the individual is rewarded in the next life. Buddhists emerged from that philosophy observing that to evolve to excellence, a life could be completed by bypassing returning to a life of struggle (reincarnation) associated with living. The real opportunity can be had by all if you realize life requires you to be the best transcending to greatness, "forgive, love, and lift others up!" Essentially be positive, attract like-minded and be a beam of bright light in the dark. No one has it easy, fighting the blockage in your thoughts that are limiting. Interference stands between you simply achieving your goal. Look beyond, harness the positive energy "begin now" there is never a better time than this moment. Do you know why you're here on this planet? Do you know your identity? In a journal, write it down with today's date – now, you can begin to achieve your goal. Reverse engineer, the goal begins as if you are living the goal while working on acquiring all the parts to make it a reality.

In studying the dynamics of psychotherapy, a therapist becomes proficient in identifying what beliefs belong to them and what belongs outside of themselves. Projection is a term used when a therapist perceives the client's problem through his own familiarity. The skill of self-awareness is necessary for distinguishing assumptions or making judgments that are occurring through a bias.

A distinction between empathy that enables us to feel what the other person is living for a therapist can be a determent to providing compassion. However, the submersion of pain is not the source of healing and serves no purpose to the victim or listener. Limiting the pejorative pronouns began as a way to allow victims frequently sexually abused from identifying as their abuser. I feel the pain of my Father's abandonment; therefore, I become aggressive, more masculine to project, or act out the struggle of not being able to stop the travesty. Many alternative genders have emerged as a transference for the endured suffering. The real victor will be to love authentically. Where does one learn after being conditioned to the only type of sexuality they have been accustomed to?

The way in which we experience sexuality involves intellectual, spiritual, admiration, physical, emotional, romance, erotic. A long tradition gives merit to biological choice as one of the ways in which love interest is sought in responding to a nation that pigeon noses gender biology would be of no concern. To remove the stigma of race and gender, we no longer can use antiquated scientific classifying methods for the animal kingdoms order. Proponents that go against order must first attempt to change the traditions of how we understand science for chaos to exist. Once a system of linguistics is removed, society will no longer have a means of understanding, what is left is communicating by semantics. The government's overreach begins at the point of getting involved with how we choose who we are (identity) and how one chooses who they love. Thomas Sowell, (Uncommon Knowledge Now, Discrimination and Disparities with Thomas Sowell, retrieved December 9, 2019) shows the deteriorating individual identity is contributing to the highest rates of adolescent suicide in American history. Disparate Impact is a coined term made by jargon lawyers that exploit groups for sympathetic cost value. Similar to creating a cost value to be accepted, students are being brainwashed and harmed.

Woodrow Wilson designed the biggest racist open-door immigration policy intended to justify victimization for a bigger protective government. Good intentions do not deliver results for those intended but hide money for the bureaucrats to disguise themselves based on compassion. Confusion is a barterer; it is a tactic of deceit. It seeks to create disorder, ambiguity, and rebellion. Indeed, the powerful seek to take over through legislation appearing to look like that which it is not. Sexual Choice has taken the lives in the form of suicides, increasing by 46% (Brown, David, The Growing Epidemic of Suicide Among Men,

Epoch Times, November 7, 2019, A14). Another 3 million die from HIV disease, since the sexual diversity push, which began in the '80s. If that didn't help, we had feminism pushing women to forsake men as unnecessary components to childbearing. That toll has loaded the jails with angry, rebellious identity starved children raised without the loving hand of affection and lack of discipline provided to counterparts raised in a two-parent home.

All while more self-inflicted government take over health insurance equally destroying lives to cash in the biggest revenue business pain management. Healthcare killed anyone who dared to use it. Prescription is a masterful business model developed to keep a subscription-based customer as a money-rich scheme that trades addictive, controlling substances for life.

I should know I am a single Mom engrained with these lies through higher education. The more education, the more opportunity for mind control. It is unfair to cheat a child of the security given raised in a family devoted to love and support. The policymakers would have you believe you are the enemy if you get married and work hard to provide for your family. The government wants to replace love and provide for the collective good. Will you give them your children to indoctrinate? After the most beautiful moment in my life, my son's birth at the first office visit to the doctor who delivered my son told me I was depressed; I was suffering postpartum. He assured me Zoloft would make me happier and help with the new life I was experiencing. My son's birth was December 14, 1993. I couldn't get out of the hospital because the nurse told me I didn't press the Morphine drip button. I knew I had to get out of the hospital before I was turned into an addict.

I packed myself up, grabbed my baby, and walked out. The hospital was having a crisis! Next, the lovely Doctor wanted to cheat me of being fully present for the best part of being a woman becoming a Mother! It did not stop my friends all ended up using prescriptions with terrible outcomes for their children and families. One mother became a sex fiend even deadbolted her children in their rooms while she engaged in curing her insatiable appetite.

Children were the target during the elementary school years by prescribing controlled substances as medication. Ritalin was prescribed to help children calm down to become a better student. Later, High school and college students needing more focus passed Adderall around like a cup of coffee. The opium crisis ensured that if any survived a horrible upbringing with pill-aholic single parents, they would die by another round of Dr. Jekyll potions paid for by tax dollars.

The Center for Urban Renewal and Education (CURE) suggests the reason for a systemic political shift are the children raised by single Mothers, teen pregnancy, school propaganda, sexual manipulation, and a loss of morality that has contributed to the chaos, instability ultimately causing institutionalization and early death.

I am looking to the agencies created to keep us in a false reality. For instance, the center for the disease will never publish the cause for the high suicide rate among the LBGT community. Creating an emotional twist to promote gender confusion, the government agency disguises the death toll labeling for various reasons.

A bystander paying attention after years of being sold as a "social justice" campaign can compare years of intervention to cure a problem to years prior to rectifying the disparity. It appears that whenever the government gets involved, the cost of the problem is paid with lives. Serving the underclass among us, for those deprived of justice, means unlike a chameleon when our position is to defend a baby who is reliant that we, as developed humans, will do the right thing? How can we punish those among us with no voice and enact legislation that directly harms us? The US District Court for the District of Columbia stands in the way of justice. He is seeking to protect inmates on death row to be absolved while sentencing the innocent babies to death. It is feckless, cowardly not to be accountable to a powerless fetus. No wonder the other Communist nations think Americans are soft.

Try smoking or littering in Shanghai. Destroying property that belongs to the totalitarian regimes which are owned by the State is punishable by death. An American while traveling in China defaced property, he was jailed while imprisoned his body parts were harvested until he was released back to Warmbier parents, to Otto's demise (Fang, Frank, Chinese Regime likely manipulated organ donation data, study finds, Epoch Times, 11/27/2019, A1, and A11).

Fairtrade is at the pinnacle of citizens' freedom. A country built on free markets doesn't praise lawbreakers. Otherwise, it will continually reward an underclass that seeks to take from hard-working Americans that, unlike Socialized countries, have the untouchable protected class at the top, and the rest of society is left to fight it out with no winners except the existing rulers. Recent immigration laws have been allowed to exist like the wild west. The chaos only helps bring people reliant on subsidies given to them as a prize for breaking laws for which citizens would be punished. Distributing wealth from the bottom classes to take care of non-citizens is an intentional design to rob them from competing with the privileged educations, private clubs, and expensive lifestyles of the wealthy.

Martha Walters Oregon Supreme Court Justice sought to protect illegals from coming into America unannounced. Evidently, as long as we can raise taxes, the American people will be happy to have the law broken, and for those families that climb over the wall stealing their way into this country, don't expect it will end there. That is who they are, and they disrespect laws. Laws that allow asylum would reveal the laundry lists of crime.

If Judge Walters has her way, she will eliminate, prevent, and stop ICE enforcement dedicated to providing a secure environment for the hard-working, law-abiding good-hearted American folks. It seems like not only are we being told to hate Protestants, men, heterosexuals, voters but ourselves included.

If you don't think you are disposable to the politicians, public schools, and media, the evidence does not lie. Their collaboration to promote sexual diversity against a silent health epidemic that conservatively predicts 1.9 million infected with a transmittable HIV disease (CDC.gov 18002323646, recording 12/14/2019) instead of creating policies designed to keep Americans safe that would warn the public instead of cheerleading to engage in a sexual lifestyle that spreads infections is proof.

The STATE of STDs in the United States

in 2017

THE NATION EXPERIENCES STEEP AND SUSTAINED STD INCREASES.

1.7 million
CASES OF CHLAMYDIA
22% increase since 2013

555,608
CASES OF GONORRHEA
67% increase since 2013

30,644
CASES OF SYPHILIS
76% increase since 2013

LEARN MORE AT: www.cdc.gov/std/

WORLDWIDE DEATHS THIS YEAR

1/1/2020 - 4/1/2020
https://www.worldometers.info/

10,670,908 Deaths from Abortion
2,807,806 Deaths from Starvation
2,061,853 Deaths from Cancer
1,254,997 Deaths from Smoking
422,032 Deaths from HIV/AIDS
338,886 Deaths from Traffic Accidents
269,209 Deaths from Suicide
246,250 Deaths from Malaria
211,416 Deaths from unclean drinking water
122,062 Deaths from Seasonal Flu
46,491 Deaths from Coronavirus

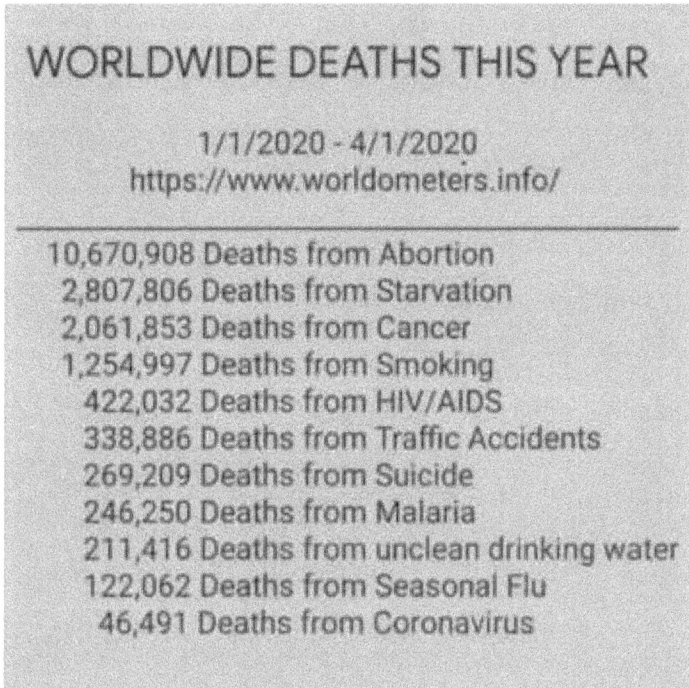

The government needs you to be sick, the sicker the public is the more government programs, and additional money to fund programs benefit self-interests, big medicine, and selling America short while jobs and manufacturing are shipped overseas. In jeopardy are American employee job security increasing public dependency on the state. This reliance on big government is leaving us sick if not dead for profit.

I am a runner. In many races that I attend, there are children running. Learning to challenge yourself to run a race allows you to rely on yourself. It elevates your mood, promoted by an endorphin surge. Serotonin is increased, and camaraderie with other runners is forged into a unifying force. Often, endurance despite physical pain reminds me of how to physically appreciate the pain because I am fortunate to have legs. The racers share stories of determination; many are cancer survivors, and many participants run as a tribute for a life cut short. I always say if anyone wanted to trade a way out of problems for someone else's problems, they would keep their own. No matter what the challenge is, mental agility in a race has a way of leveraging setbacks that people overcome.

Recognizing the food industry compromised America's health contributing to obesity, inflammation, and disease. People are skeptical about their food; the microscope is out people are avoiding foods laden with additives. Vying for real food, the culprit is the processed, artificial, and synthetic foods causing obesity and disease. I have taken my political view to take apart government influence in the food manufacturing industry.

I began by maintaining the life of Vegetables and Beans for a nutrient-dense option in the prepared food space. I was challenged to solve this injustice by inventing a food product to meet the new lifestyles of busy Moms that fell culprit to the processed foods with little to no nutrition – running the first round through a kitchen top production to measure out weights of ingredients methods of preparation and best cooking tools to maintain nutrient density. My first test round began in Palo Alto, California. I conducted the research in a food lab to ensure that my idea of a flexible, easy-to-transition prepared ready-to-eat artificials free food as possible. It was there that I learned the very food degradation is the process that all food products underwent as public safety.

I was told by professionals in the food manufacturing industry that are responsible for government MRE to Wendy's Chili and beans, that food had to be dead so it does not have any foodborne bacteria that would lead to a health hazard. We calculated the internal temperature of the particulates of food deep into the center of the pouch to ensure nothing posed a potential health risk.

While I watch the food get killed, so did my invention of maintaining maximum nutrition. Apparently, the health risk was the lack of beneficial amino acid chain structures that were destroyed. The importance of riding our bodies of disease is to digest beneficial vitamins and minerals from live food sources equivalent to that which is grown from the earth. Vegetables in its most natural state protect the body from inflammation, the leading contributor to disease. I traveled to the opposite coast within the country to learn I would be contributing to the problem of unhealthy food. I would spend the next three years finding, creating, developing, and producing a food product that did not exist meant GotMeals single pack vegetables revolutionized a new category.

I traveled by and far to bring a pH balanced food in a BPA free pouch that delivered beneficial "living nutrition." It meant this new category had competed with the multi-million-dollar space in the refrigeration aisle where everyday consumables are found, i.e., milk, cheese, eggs, drinks, and GotMeals. I incorporated a new technology tested in Ohio at a University originating in Sweden and used in India, Italy, Korea, and the Netherlands.

A local food manufacturer opened a facility to use high-pressure processing. The time was right to merge advanced methods with precision quality plant-based foods. I attended the first unveiling recalculated initial flavors using ingredients that created a symbiosis among the ingredients, for the conduit and consumption. A specialized microwave or boil pouch ensure delivered Ayurvedic prepared meal option for a healthy choice. From 2008 to 2019, the facility of operation and product labeling has received FDA Food Facility Registered, The State Department of Consumer Protection License, The City Department of Health, Organic Certification, Non-GMO certification, Serve Safe Manager certification, Trademark, and product liability Insurance as the housekeeping items.

To date we have explored the market growing into prepared meal kits including a trademarked "SpiceBall," Frozen Vegetable Purée BabyFood, MicroNutri dried fruits, vegetables, and herbs, Human-grade Dog Food Fresh or Frozen with sea vitamins and minerals and Medicinal Chips projection launch in late 2020, made for high protein snack with the benefits of eatable botanicals.

I rented space from the Banquet Facility I founded in New Haven, "The BallRoom," after receiving a degree in Hotel and Restaurant Management from the College of Boca Raton, aka Lynn University, in 1990. The commercial kitchen would provide the small-batch kitchen to commercialize GotMeals into a business that supported hiring employees.

The job listing posted on the local "Craigs List" and the interviews began to hire the first production crew and the manuals for kitchen production, protocol, vendor order and receiving, accounting, packaging, tracking, supplies, accounting, were executed.

Hitting the local markets in an electric vehicle, keeping the food in refrigerator temperature-controlled units, the most important part of the launch was to sell, sell, sell. The new changing food delivery is ultimately where we felt the maximum pulse to catapult into bypassing the politics of big boxes and focus on affording healthy eaters the best pricing mailed directly through delivery to the home.

With the advent of cool wraps and ice packs, shipping in an environmentally conscious footprint was achieved using minimal packaging, never losing sight of the mission fresh prepared holistic food eliminating food waste, and developing healthy eating habits conveniently. Listening to the public and watching trends is integral to meeting the demand of the market. Like navigating through life, learning skills that can translate to every facet of your personal and professional acumen must be harnessed from the masters and tweaked with the unique foresight to imprint your endeavor to advance civilization. Sometimes pursuing your dreams has no guarantees but slow and steady wins the race.

"They who can give up essential liberty to obtain a little temporary safety deserve neither liberty nor safety."

– Benjamin Franklin

Chapter 7
Trader

Have you ever thought about what will happen if China overtakes the US economy?

At a rally celebrating the 70th anniversary of the founding of the People's Republic of China, Xi Jinping said, "*No force can shake the status of this great nation.*" If you accept that China will, in about ten years' time, become the world's largest economy, it is hard to see any set of circumstances that will stop that from happening. If things go really wrong for China, then this could take a few more years than that. But it is going to happen in the foreseeable future, so we had better get used to it.

A point that reminds me of why it is important never to give up is the Chinese are coming. Americans may have forgotten that theirs is the land of opportunity. At our feet is the development of prosperity felt in many industrialized advanced technological societies. China is aware of the formula to excellence, but as for America, it has gotten complacent, to preserving the good fortune our great countryman lived and died to create for us. A poignant saying, someone's misfortune is someone else's fortune. The repurposing industry knows this by salvaging someone's dumping into another use of garbage that is then reused. That is what is becoming of American industry and agriculture products.

The chart below illustrates what will occur when America gives up. There is a measure of one man's loss, is another man's gain. I hear the debate quite frequently that if we allow immigrants into this country that they would vote in a way that would disadvantage one party over another. Clearly, in the United States, Democrats believe they can win elections by creating a population to vote them into government. However, many immigrants that are coming into the United States of America are fleeing totalitarian regimes.

These new voters understand the opportunities that await them. They had lost all to a corrupt economy that exploits the labor of the many for the enrichment of the few. There are many descriptions of what socialism is. I don't think it occurs to the typical American voter that interchangeably, communism is socialism. Voters from countries, if allowed to migrate to the United States, would never vote

Democratic. Socialism may have a good advantage, but everyone must contribute by working, and those that work hard are entitled to keep their rewards. In countries with a larger population, it becomes a burden on economics; the greater the population, the more people that cannot work; the more people take from the government, the more money must be collected to subsidize the incapable and the non-working.

If there is not enough money to take care of their families, how can socialism work? Will working voters, vote to burden themselves with more hours of work and less money to take home? The prospect of doing less work for higher wages is the promise of most labor unions. School administrations and government employees are aware of doing less; it is how each succeeding budget year demands more dollars. Be careful – less is less. The work ethic brought by this game is setting the way for defeat. The spider web entangles by rewarding corrupt bureaucracies that exchange a payoff by teachers' union dues. School classrooms ought to be no place for politics, but government-run schools are enmeshed in partisan politics.

US trade with China

US trade deficit with China has soared since 1985

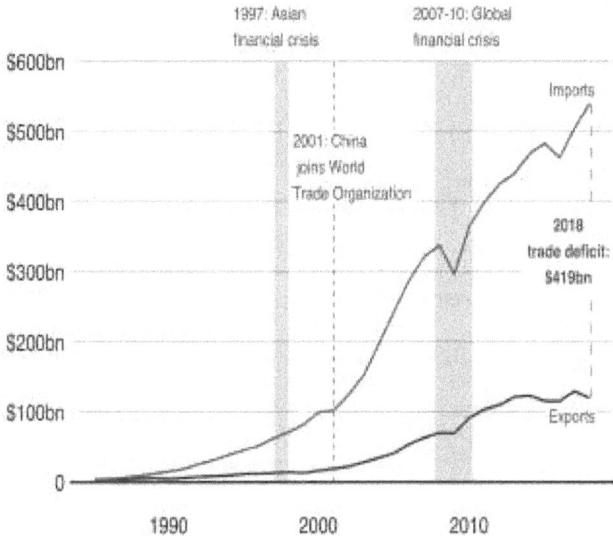

Source: US Census — BBC

Poor manufacturing production and higher product costs open the door for foreign sourcing of those products. Organized labor's drive to raise workers' wages in any other nation would be welcomed; the model for union work can be replicated in South America, Mexico, China, where workers have no rights. Simply put, unions gather up the wage earners' spoils for the Supreme Party. It is a model that other Communist nations are already using: the workers are controlled by the government they work for. A poor work ethic leaves room for takeovers. And for that matter, the Chinese own many investments, not to mention a trillion-dollar loan in the US (Renee Wilde, NPR, American soil is increasingly foreign-owned, 5/27/2019.)

In the United States, the top 1% of earners pay 97.3% of income taxes. 80% of taxes are paid by middle and upper incomes combined to provide government assistance to the bottom income group. Class conflict is perpetuated rhetoric from politicians pitting public and private sector workers against each other. Bureaucrats and union workers have to put skin in the game; the private sector businessmen and women like myself have not only their epidermis but their vital organs in the game.

We stand united to protect children, mothers, the elderly, and the disabled. But that is not what is at force here; the deceit is to cripple blacks, whites, and anyone who raises their hand to take services. Those services put you and your family on the radar of generational dependency. Since 1940, 27% of receiving social services has become a way of navigating through the system. The sicker you are, the more money the bureaucrats bring in for their programs. The social service motto, "build it, and they will come." Are you familiar with the Eagle's song "Hotel California," "you can enter, but you can never leave." The United States is on the precipice of advancing or declining. While the rich pay 97.3% of the taxes, 80% goes to the bottom tax tier (Phil, Gramm and John F. Early, The Truth about income inequality, 12,3,2019). In the movie Crazy Rich Asians, the movie, while entertaining, is surreal. The United States is not as advanced as we think. As many practice resistances the determent to capitalism here at home, there is ample room available for advancements, conversely not the United States of America's.

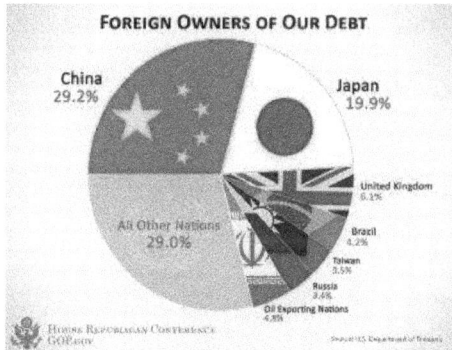

The advancement for citizens or nationals to own a piece of their country, their businesses, and their farms. Unfortunately, the foreign buyers are getting control because Americans have stopped achieving the dream to own land, homes, and businesses. Looking at the evidence makes it apparent that principal players are selling Americans out to China. The government shouldn't be in the people's way, but it is taking over the small guy's ability to keep some of the profit without devoting more than a month's pay for federal taxes, another month pay for state taxes, another month for municipal taxes, and then insurance the margins for eight months of revenues must be worth the gamble to open a small business. Remaining is a discouraged employer left with little to manage paychecks plus pay for employee incentives.

Small businesses are becoming an anomaly drowned in red tape. It proves out if you want to be rich, do what rich people do. If you want to be poor, believe the less you do, the government programs will take care of you. Do you feel the heartfelt government is worried about you? Government programs will be tapped out if this belief that the 27% plus top tax tier will have enough money to foot the bill for all undocumented families taking from the non-workers, disabled, elderly, and dependent children and mothers. Programs that pay for services are all-inclusive medical, housing, comprehensive child care, elderly caregivers and hospitalization, nursing homes, transportation, public utilities, schooling, food, and monthly income. The "nanny state" is "Big Daddy "the consequence in recent times is the demise of thriving economies Argentina, Brazil, Venezuela, and Cuba. There is no mechanism that collects from the rich and gives to the poor that is successful. Without capitalism, most people give up, as seen in San Francisco; most homeless were once entrepreneurs in the technology sector only to have given up. Capitalism gives everyone ownership in a piece that collectively makes a whole.

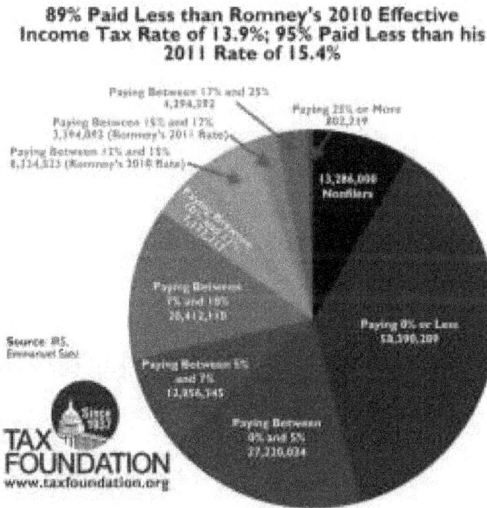

89% Paid Less than Romney's 2010 Effective Income Tax Rate of 13.9%; 95% Paid Less than his 2011 Rate of 15.4%

It is similar to Bitcoin in that a piece belongs to everyone for it to work. It is the collective parts that make the

Democratic- Republic function. This instrument best prevents wealth from being held in the hands of a few. What happens to quality? Judging from research development and technological advancement, capitalism fares the best economic system. Distribution of resources somehow obscures progress or the race to become the best. Competition is a force to be reckoned with. The wolf is always at the door. Staying ahead faster, smarter, better is guaranteed in a competitive economy. The discussion leads to the high price attributed to the greatness that is corruption.

Ralph Wald Emerson said, *"It is one of those beautiful compensations of life that no one can sincerely try to help another without helping himself."*

The downfall of mankind is greed. Is there any drug known to man that can cure avarice? Are we to harness gain in the light of all things being equal? The fundamental benevolence is heavily reliant on each member doing their best with no particular difference. Is it correct to believe all resources are endless, capable of supporting all, with no one wanting any more than the collective good? This removes kickbacks, backroom deals, political action committees, and lobbyists squiring for priority while pandering a one size fits all. Do we all want the same things? Are we all the same or do we all do different things, are we all different? The dynamic is we are human, which makes our story the same. Tracing the beginning of man back to the Middle East, all descendants are the same, but we all want different things.

Would you agree materialism separates us from non-materialistic? What do we do in a society of sameness, how do the shoppers live futile lives? Or do we make them conform to do without? Do you want to live rudimentary lives because we despise greed? Is that the answer to the inequality of social justice? A legal system designed to prosecute the unlawful is the only code of ethics we have for justice. Has it not worked for the United States? It has. However, it has to the success of all world powers.

Every act of kindness allows the individuals a conscious awareness to appreciate what they have earned and the desire to give back. The Yin Yang Jingoist philosophy believes every time you give of yourself to help others, you get at least as much back in return. When the State steps in to take away the process of "giving," it reduces man's futility imposing a demand or an obligation without fostering empathy, compassion, the problem for the individual to resolve, not the state. A false narrative creates a false perception of social justice. Creating a footprint to become self-sufficient is a parable used in the Bible if you teach a man to fish he will eat for a lifetime if you give a man a fish he will learn to ask for a fish. Whether it is the environment, family/non-family, schooling, hard knocks, media, etc. what becomes imprinted on us occurs by familiarity. Did you ever hear that familiarity breeds contempt? There is a passage in the Bible, by the way, why don't people read the Bible and find out for themselves what is in the oldest book ever written. The Bible can only make you better. It has been the single greatest influencer in any reader's life. The Bible eludes us to protect ourselves from impurity. How do we become impure defiling our bodies, sex out of marriage, taking in pornography, slander, gossiping, stealing, not keeping the Sabbath a holy day, and more actions taken in by our eyes and ears that subtly become part of our being? How to resist being consumed by harm in life is emphasized. No, I do not have the secret potion, but reading the Bible will open your eyes to become discerning to a false narrative and avoid being left in the wilderness.

Putting on the Holy Spirit's armor is recognized as protection to a temptation that may create a life of wastefulness, one in which you chase after the wind. The opposite is true if you allow yourself to read what the Bible offers cover to cover. Then you are equipped, as said – to fight the good fight.

The groups that once blamed corporations for greed and corruption are seeing the golden revolver of distrust turned against themselves. Congress's trust had dropped from a time when an unassuming public in times past use to believe. All levels of organized trust are witnessing dramatic declines the media, law enforcement, medicine, banking, and academic leaders trust (Scott Man, Lead others with a trust mindset, C8, 12/5/2019). Seeking out the truth is an active and reoccurring investment that educates us rather than blind faith. The most rudiment argument is a religion based on faith isn't finding the truth relative. Based on the gut, instinct, and experimental learning weighs rational decisions and readjust in a continual effort to search for meaning.

It is screwed up, but most individuals surrender to guidance after life becomes abysmal. Living in honesty is up to you to break through the false rhetoric and open up to the vulnerability of allowing yourself to be different from the conditioning of the bigger group. I got news for you. You wouldn't still be reading if you think this is not going to be beneficial to find out what you want to know, **what is the truth about myself in relationship to my existence.**

Let go of rhetoric; once the in-groups' trust has been broken, a new beginning will emerge. You can be what you were fully intended to be if you go back to the beginning and find your God's voice. That is an inner voice that guides you in a relationship where your faith is led into an authentic personal relationship with your creator.

Jesus made you in your mother's womb. He knows you intimately, every fiber, every cell "I knew you in your mother's womb before you were born" (Mathew 5:78). "I know every hair on your head" (Luke 12:1723). God loves you more than you know, even more than you will allow him to love you, abundantly, endlessly, and forever. So, go on the best journey, let go of what society has imprinted upon you and take a venture to oneness with Your Lord and Savior.

How did we grow so far from our childlike being? The authentic person pure and loved is waiting to shine! Take off the false and put on the truth. It may hurt, but you already have become familiar with learning to trust. Run the race to win the challenges of self-discovery, self-discipline, and persistence. There is an old Chinese proverb that says, "You cannot prevent the birds of sorrow from flying over your head, but you can prevent them from building a nest in your hair." Bridging trust allows the individual to share in a unifying vision for a higher performance. Trusting the work you do serves a purpose. It fortifies the country, the culture, business, health and well-being builds society, but the individual must choose to be sick or healthy. Contemplation, meditation and self-reflection will guide you right. The most fun times in my life took me off track because the noise and distractions kept me away from the introspection that only comes with quiet time. I moved forward through the confusion because I never want to be lost without meaning again.

Recently, while at a food show in South Florida for the company, GotMeals, which I began in 2008. I had talked with over 1,000 people, some mocking the unusual product concept, some authentically interested in good nutrition, and overall, I was struck by the masses of people whose value is in the moment. Many were there because they had nothing to do; many looked at me like I was trying to get something out of them. I was there for their benefit. It is my purpose to improve the quality of people's nutrition not to detract.

In the last days of the fair, people with the most horrid stories began rushing at me, pouring out their nightmares. The last two women made an impact as it relates to twins in comparison to distinguish in their words "it is not true what they say that twins are alike."

Two separate women within moments of each other brought me a message. It resonated in application to the preceding chapter "false illusions." The scientists, educational institutions, and media be it Hollywood or print inundate American society with a false message (narrative). These mothers learned a lesson that contrasted with a lie that almost took the life of their children. The first mother was very hesitant to call it Schizophrenia, but the medicine told me another story. This mom began that the GotMeals Meal Kits were perfect for her son in college. She digressed that while her philosophy is to eat organically, she had to accept that her son requires medication. She questioned how twins could be so different from each other? Where they both were raised in the same environment? Initially, she stated it must be organic. The question is are we a product of our environment, or are we organically pre-dispositioned? Recently, my son thanked me for the environment I provided for him to grow up in. When my son was in his twenties at a time in life, I have been told about men that he could be filled with uncertainty such as what do I want to do for the rest of my life, how do I get to where I want to go, and where do I want to go and with whom am I going to get there with? I am probably transferring these questions from my predilection of young adulthood.

Ultimately, he concluded that while many in his peer group had not been supportive, he would have expected. He related to the indifference as deriving from the environment of experiences to trust beyond the in group. He said what every mother hopes to hear one day, "Mom, you always supported me" I guess if someone doesn't have that in their home, they never know how to be supportive to others. I admire my son because he is profound. Throughout his life, he has expounded larger than life wisdom. He does not talk much; the quiet type an observer. Speaking less and listening more is a talent for some, it comes naturally. I am not a good listener; however, I am analytic. We possess gifts for us to use, but only if we recognize what the gifts are and how can we use them. Becoming aware of identity can be synthesized clearly if a parent reinforces a child's gifts. Note that I did not say talent. A gift is an innate it unconsciously exists but to manifest its potential to recognize its uniqueness; it can be used miraculously in life; thus, the name "gift."

A talent is playing the piano, being athletic, and a sculptor. The message from the next mom at the fair makes an innuendo that she goes everywhere with her daughter, who is a recovering drug abuser. The mom had recently found the daughter's friend Zack dead on the floor in her apartment. The mom went to meet the family of Zack to discover a twin sister.

She explained her daughter was with her girlfriend at the fair, and she has dedicated herself to being around her all the time to prevent her from reusing drugs. Zack was becoming a male; her twin sister proved to her the environment caused the gender confusion for her daughter's generation. Apparently, a brutal murder was in revenge for a violent rape in which Zack avenged on his sister's behalf. Sentenced to a year in jail, the mom learned while visiting the twin sister of what she believed proved experiences make us who we are.

Predators that harm one person causes harm to all of us. The original act of violence caused gender confusion, anger, revenge, and innocent loss of life. The value of honesty, integrity, dependability, reliability can only be practiced in an environment of trustworthiness.

I know if the Bible tells us it is wise for us to keep away from that which will corrupt us, we need to believe and act upon making our lives live accordingly. Good begets that which is good. My friends not only steer clear of evil; you must pray against it and curse it immediately. In Christ, we are given the gift to have power over evil. How do you use it? Well, it comes in three's a young peppy, joyous full of love girl sixteen told me her best friend ended her life one year ago. She stated we were inseparable; we were even going to the prom together.

How well we deal with pressure was the overarching theme extolling as apart each of these stories. Life can be difficult how anyone can get through the hard times without Gods enormity to deliver us in grief to a statement every believer accounts, "It is for a reason that this happened, the lesson is..." Every believer knows God brings it, and God takes it away. I am always overjoyed by a believer's faith or, as George Harrison sang this too shall pass, a verse taken from Ecclesiastics. Once you know the Bible, the origin of existence and everything above and below the sun parallels. The Hindus teach a rich man must have done well; the wealth is his reward.

How then does anyone change and become fluid to circumstances? A person is limited by teaching that believes you get what you deserve. I met a young college girl studying to become an Anthropologist. I conveyed my political views to abortion, socialism, minimum wage, taxes, education, unions, health accounts, and education. The conversation gave insight into a construct that, similar to Hinduism, perpetuates entrapment.

A cycle in many philosophies, religion, and culture with little provocations to believe anything different. The Anthropologist spent a study abroad in Romania. I pried a thought-provoking question, "does your generation think the government really cares if we are healthy or not?" She answered No, but people don't make enough money, and the minimum wage needed to be $15.00. The problem is that companies do not pay their workers. She offered an example, Jeff Bezos, the owner of Amazon, treats his employees without breaks; they eat at their desks. Jeff Bezos is a Liberal. I am pretty sure the bigger government protects the giant contributors, adding most of Seattle and Silicone Valley have chummed together, all guilty of telling you to hate the rich. What is really meant is the group that controls the information does not want anything or anyone to stop them.

The rich are you and me; it is classism, the one thing lobbyist, elites, and Hollywood invite to their gala parties, is inequality. The parties all of us are kept out from attending. So much for the common people. The common American is being left out of the extravagant party! I predict Anarchy within the next ten years, I believe drugging American children, rewriting history books, and impenetrable biased news has played out as far as it could go. We are as a society killing ourselves, pills, alcohol, and innocent life for a few seconds of recreational sex. Mothers that are shown as children love, self-respect, and family unity have a better outcome as adults with their own families. Without the women at the head of the household, we are living with a weak foundation. The leaders of corporations that are unsupported as boys consequentially, they cannot take their place as protectors of the family, instead they exploit power. Women are displaced by polarization of femininity with an alternate angry message. How can a society become disrupted to a contentious message that boys no longer have an epistemological evolution into Fathers or that women's development no longer is Motherhood? A crisis of gender roles has been manufactured, ultimately convoluting a design prognosticated in table 34. Designing androgyny has altered identity, confidence, and is paralyzing teens, ultimately causing a mass loss of life[14]. Unconventional genders disrupt tradition only to be a disaster. The old way preserved life at all costs.

Human preservation promotes life. It is a worthy cause to choose to give children a stable home providing nourishing food, and parents that enforce disciple even when it hurts the parent more than the good it does the child. Somewhere the message of child raising got monopolized to indulging bad behavior. We are being sold a story that the circumstances could change based on resources outside of our ability. Apparently, what limits us is not a religion, culture, or biases

---

[14]Ann, P. & et al. (2014). Suicide Attempts among Transgender and Gender Non-Conforming Adults. The Williams Institute. Retrieved from: https://queeramnesty.ch/docs/AFSP-Williams-Suicide-Report-Final.pdf

to better social order. The limitations are not trusting in ourselves. Each has the freedom to eat healthier garden vegetables and fruits are free. Individuals that practice saving 1/3 of their paycheck build a future. The message, for everyone parents and children, is to take control by investing in themselves. The media, Hollywood, and the government will not give you an advanced degree, a home, a car, or take care of you when you're sick and old. The wealthy individuals learn how to save, plan, and invest in a secure future from their parent's beginning in childhood.

I predict future happiness for Americans if they can prevent the government from wasting the labors of the people under the pretense of taking care of them.

-Thomas Jefferson

Chapter 8
Homelessness

Charities provide most of the social services. Organized programs, both a religious food pantry and soup kitchens and municipalities, build shelters with vocational programs, and the alternative is still begging. We live in America, not Venezuela. Beggars live better in the US than Kings and Queens in the 1st century.

Victimhood compromises too many lives. Yes, life, poor or rich, is HARD! It is about how one navigates the struggle and the choices one makes. Frivolous behaviors may roll the tire further down the road but even a wealthy person meets the same result, the tire must be fixed. However, the inevitable flaw cannot be masked, and this is why rich or poor that a waste of talent will lead to nothingness.

The appreciation level of a simple source of water has lost its value literally drowned out by convenience of the water bottle. Disposable plastic containers that afford the garish loss of value for the bottle to be reused as it is in Uganda. Ugandans keep Rubbermaid bowls and water bottles a lifetime and share the communal meal by washing from a pale of water the limited supply of plastic plates and cups for the next person to use. We have become a society that believes a peanut comes from a jar with a dancing peanut wearing a top hat.

I worked as a social worker in an economically diverse city, Bridgeport, Connecticut. The "system" that appears to serve the marginalized in reality is oppressive by its very nature. The government-run agencies are limited with few resources. Instead, the insurance monies are capitalized for budgets supporting operations and the bureaucracy's employment, the "system" which exists for the middle class to dispense programs for the wayward. The judicial system intervened in becoming an arbitrator in a society that no longer is able to communicate amongst family members. The system creates jobs to manage people who forgot how to apply for work, forget how to forgive, and become self-centered, and hostile. Money is the reward for causing harm to a once cherished relationship.

The war between vital relationships is the micro picture to a macro problem that repeats itself by taking and robbing us all. Instead of dividing up assets imposed by a State facilitator, the emphasis should be about the individual ability to be empowered. By supporting access to education lives have been changed amongst inmates. Apparently, jail eliminates distractions causing one to invest in themselves and change the trajectory of their lives. The higher education model works to enrich and impact self-worth. It is a commodity that can never be taken away! But instead to no fault of the State government, the system cleans up as individuals give away their liberty and inheritance refusing to access education.

Mental illness is a measure of the good that local services achieve. My work as a social work intern dealt with dual diagnoses. A dual diagnosis was no fault of the individual, functioning members of society are sympathetic towards. The cost of services is referred to as primary cost, auxiliary cost, and ancillary costs. Together cost for an individual receiving these services can well exceed $24,000 a month per person. Medication alone rang up for tax payers at a tune of $6,000 a month. Shocked? There is a "system" that the State budgets serve to meet the needs of the disadvantage of society. The wealthier the state, the better the programs offered to meet the needs of its functional and nonfunctional citizens. Likewise, towns block the ills of society by hiking up property values, punitive laws to penalize panhandling and solicitors, building state of the art schools and municipal parks, boathouses, recreational facilities, exotic stores to provide their insulated worldview. Their excess creates no room for going without, the local Starbucks pushes out $7.00 plastic nonsense beverages to reward the midday cognitive dissonance. Obnoxious behaviors are played by postmodernists who have compassion for the poor but are 7 degrees removed. Insulated by sentiments that believe in government extortion to rectify the ills of society. The disenfranchised are receiving services in a system layered with "programs" which offer those that want municipal services a place to get their needs met.

The fact is a segment of society cannot live without these supports. Profoundly, a benevolence that their greedy independent community members forget. Pushed off as a tax solution cure while indulging in air-conditioning, Whole Foods Market, Tesla, and collegiate excesses to blame the immaterial "Corporations," and "Racist"!!! Labels conveniently distance themselves from the disgusting disposable proclivities that mount plastic, Styrofoam walls barricading them from the travesty they accuse some abstract corporation from perpetuating. I lived in such a community outside of New York. The liberal elite made six figures in Manhattan and ran to their mansions in the suburbs, isolating their family from the compassion they espouse. Often the cure to move to towns no one but people like themselves could afford. A homogenous community with elite educations, entitled to all the accouterments comfort and prestige, could bestow anyone. Yes, give to the poor, raise taxes was the chant. A listener might hear this as an empathetic plea for equality, a solution that directly gave their money back to its beneficiaries.

A conservation or rationing was beneath their dignity as the orders for food spewed from their lips, glasses of pretentious wine poured to their unquenched desires and when they glamour themselves among the social class of their kind the food was left on the plates to dispose of without any clue of conspicuous consumption., An entitled group of vulgar pandering delusional Hippocrates ! However – the best system in the world. Their money allowed for their pleasures and the needs of the less fortunate – both to my standard, excessive.

A country that takes care of the weakest elderly, mentally ill, children, is a compassionate society. However, it works it does. Maybe the administrators skim of the top, maybe the wealthy indulge themselves and maybe the social services allow some to advance and other to live carelessly. Be it as it is civilization changes have markedly witnessed the climb of women and blacks out from the inclusion of the weak, pivoting as a society to empower the disenfranchised of previous generations. It is no mistake that Sweden and Russia have the highest alcoholic rate. The United States is the only democratic republic left in which it provides for society weakest tempered with the balance for individual satisfaction.

Groups are kept indifferent by exploiting self-interest hidden by blaming or spewing out the corrective measures. Asking a homeless person if they would like to live in a building or the National park would look more like meeting the individual where they are. I recently asked a couple of San Francisco residents if they would offer the National parks to provide refuge for the current epidemic of "outdoorsman" that live on the streets in tents, their reply, "No, they will ruin the parks!"

Cronyism, patriotism, and corruption pull at the fabric of envy, destroy the next guy to ensure pedagogy. Bestowing unearned privileges as an inheritance to children to attend the best schools, meet the right people, and land a job with a well-connected influential "group perpetuate exclusion." Every dominating proponent superficially collaborates, for their absolution offering "health care programs" as a right, enjoy another pill, kill those who you pretend to help at the knee of the embedded payoffs to corporate insurance companies and legislatures cronyism. Paying taxes as a human token to those who can't help themselves divide the privileged class but pacify the marginalized.

The "White Privilege Guilt" has no one to blame for the voluntary agreement to set the stage for archetypal destruction that leads to depression, hopelessness, and death. The paradox is so overt it is declassified no one can hide behind "I don't know much about politics." Do you know your living? Then don't vote if you want to claim selective ignorance. Being logical, DQ. McInerny directs that of clear and effective thought to 10 habits in his book, "Being Logical: A guide to good thinking."

Deciphering storytelling may sound relative based on subjective ideas but illogical, baseless, and non-objective with verbal trickery. Ontological truth is based on logical, authentic reasoning, thought, and language just as matching an individual to the correct environment creates a symbiosis for that individual to thrive. Offering help can be a slippery slope. There once was a competent, capable, somewhat aggressive woman who understood her needs and advocated for herself. A servant found her and promised to take care of her. She held out her bottle and exclaimed, "I can't open the bottle, please remove the cap." The servant coddled her, removing the cap with a twist called enabling. The lesson the wrong environment can make us weak.

As a society, natural environments would look simple. Here is a solution to resolve nurturing families in a symbiotic manner. An Initiative to house elders and single mothers to support one another to benefit mothers, elderly, and children. It seems practical that moms could use a hand from elders with the expertise and patience for childcare. A mixed-use building is the optimal setting with a ground floor composed of retail for the employment of the parents housed within.

Housing for a six-story building includes a playscape garage with the main elevator for residence with one floor designated for child enrichment and care. Self-supporting individuals promote a healthier planet. The road to challenge the supervision of an entire gender and race was won by one little weapon; education. Equal access to having a voice eliminated the taboo that women and blacks could be disregarded. I grew up in a cultural, challenged ethnic family. Women were to serve men. The family dynamic did emphasize education. Although I navigated through a privileged private education landscape mainly Dominican, a subset of Catholic teaching reliant on nuns and priest educators. These wonderful educators are vanishing resources being replaced by technology. New methods of raising the poor have eclipsed generationally.

Taking courses at community colleges during the summer allowed me to accelerate academic credits and graduate college earlier. The public environment was different than the parochial schools. The curriculum is intense 7 subjects of study a day compared to 5 in public school. The informal behavior of walking at liberty around the school is considered a distraction. A student is quit until called upon and you better know your material. The power of the educational environment can alter the way we behave. Indoctrination became obvious to me by having the opportunity to be schooled in different methods of teaching. With the advent of new technology distant learning, paid internships, podcasts and studies abroad provide diverse experiences in education in secondary, and graduate studies.

The feminist liberation seemed to inundate my secondary and graduate formalization. That empowerment was in complete turmoil with my cultural home life customs. Here I was with an academic "liberal" worldview of empowerment in a family with an archaic conservative ideology limiting a women's role. The clash to be independent rather than subservient has been my life journey. Rivaling in a mix of a wild political view that is bold, free from indoctrination, manipulation, and promoting freedom from imposing academia, government, and media that seek to control the mind. How can anyone know what the message is tainted? "Don't believe the hype it's a put on," is a song from the '80s. An extension to Marshall McCluens, the message is n the medium. However, being inundated with biased informal and formal messages can become one's reality. How do we develop an independent view? Can you rely on discernment? Judgment is the best equipment to harness your truth. Often times, opinions seem subjected to one's reality. It does not break the cycle of false interpretations.

As far back as the Bible, a saying developed "don't kill the messenger," Evidently, civilization does not want to be told what is difficult to do. Man is inclined to do what is easy, pleasurable, a view that serves an agenda. Going along with the crowd is a satisfying feeling in itself. Doing work that is rewarded by others reinforces "Status Quo," doing what is unpopular is the purpose freedom of thought exists. Two motivators that supersede any reasoning are fear and acceptance.

Hunger is physical, and the mind can be controlled to deny hunger. Gandhi endured a hunger strike for social change. The Bible reveals fasting and prayer lead to enlightenment. Feeding hunger can be controlled. But the need to be included or the fear of being harmed, shamed, or treated inferior requires confidence developed by success in something better than ourselves. Encouraging alternative lifestyles has long been referred to as social engineering. As an entrepreneur creating a brand derives value by aligning with the "hype" of what is popular. Using tag words is optimal for searches, messaging, and staying relevant. To apply this approach to shaping individuals far penetrates qualifying factors, as seen in scholarships, grants, academic admissions, a good-faith community message designed to evoke an emotional sentiment. Selling compassion in marketing ads is given with a cost to public service messages. Be wary of messages that appeal to emotion it is bait to prey on fears, compassion or demonizing.

The past decade canonized the new ingroup chosen to receive society rewards: people of color preferably transvestites' immigrants, formally incarcerated and disabled, and every so often poor children. It may not appear that sticking it to the norm any color, any gender, any creed, any anything promotes in and of itself an offensive inclusion that is designed to eliminate anyone that does not "fit in" is that counters the end goal to gain government control of the weak the fatherless, black communities, immigrants and single women. Sell your soul, or the pied piper will not play for you.

Deconstructing begins with an alliance. Creating a war against the European ancestor males, the founders with a masculine tendency to explore, protect women and liberate. The Spanish inquisition blurred as the discovery and colonization of America. White men, religion, and liberty must be forsaken to convert the rally cry for impregnating a mirage to cause compliance. The result of discovering new lands can be seen as a continual exchange of cultures.

The schools were the perfect breeding grounds to influence gender identity ambiguity, convictions built on a distorted narrative of collective behavior that pronounces the battleground of homogeneity, heterosexuality, and individual liberty.

Enter Pop culture entrapping and dueling the mind with a subtle message of social design to benefit the Hollywood exceptional warped minds. Winning hearts and minds television was used as a social deconstruction. The Jeffersons, Brady Bunch, Oprah Winfrey, Prince of BelAir, Sponge Bob SquarePants, South Park, Ellen DeGeneres, Sex in the City, and you can add more included an ulterior motive to subtly change norms. Proactive at first, but over time change occurs breaking down old worldview. What Sitcom do you identify with having the most extreme impact on changing school behaviors? Enter streaming services Netflix, YouTube and teleservices has gone beyond the sacred racket known as the casting couch. Banished are the days of Jewish producers' control. Alfred Kinsey, a pervert botanist, convinced the government to fund a grant that paid for the molestation of children. Sex education was born from the hypothesis that humans were sexual creatures masturbating in their mother's womb.

The theory was enlarged to create sexual beings to practice unconventional proclivities without the role modeling from a heterosexual parental environment. The results were destroyed; the lab was doomed as most participating adults exploited children. Once the progressive thinkers inside the government ascertained a method to perpetuate social justice based on this research became sex education in public schools.

The plan was instituted at the college level to enter the 60's sexual revolution, then introduced in high schools and then primary grades with 2nd graders putting prophylactics on bananas. A sexually transmitted disease in the 1980's, AIDS took young men's lives as a result. My cousin Davids life, my friend Bobby and discussions were paralyzed as anti-gay or gay-bashing. A law that jeopardized Real Estate licensees was if they mentioned someone with AIDS died or lived in the house. If you want communism to prevail, silence the discussion. People that were investing in the biggest purchase of a lifetime lost the right to inquire.

It is unfair to homosexuals on their deathbeds not allowed in the hospital as extended family. That was why we needed gay marriage. That was a lie; every town hall offers a contemporaneous letter. AIDS is a lengthy disease; somewhere before the end, you write a letter giving anyone you so desire whatever privileges you wish to bequeath. The health industry has a HIPAA form (Health Insurance Portability and Accountability Act) restrictive to family members requesting auxiliary services to provide care. This may be the worst legislation. The law passed among health professionals

by telling us HIPPA protected young girls from predatorily ancestral family members. Young girls needing an abortion couldn't get their parents' consent because their parents would be upset, and the young girl's life could be endangered. Justice is to punish the family predator. Policy makers desire was to abort the baby instead of vindicating the crime. One in three to four girls and one in five to seven boys are sexually abused under the age of 18 (Mia, Fontaine, The Atlantic, America has an Incest Problem, 01,24,2013). Intentionally underreported because the legal system and the social services would not be able to handle the magnitude of housing caused by separating kin. Incest is the single biggest cause of crime, prostitution, mental illness, addictions, and alternate lifestyle. Health specialists are told by professional mandates to report abuses but unable to persecute family members on behalf of the girl as it may violate their cultural norm. HIPPA affects confidentiality the patients file requires their approval for other professionals to collaborate on a treatment plan. The client and authorized loved ones are unaware to ask to read their medical file. HIPPA punishes family care givers acting in good faith access of medical information because of the child molester.

State laws can produce inferior results from over control the Department of Motor Vehicle has lines around the building in some States. Both in Connecticut and Florida, I protested while arriving and seeing the people accepting a standard that would be aberrant had that been a private office or corporation. The people stood in line with lost hope the oppression by the 3rd Reich government, public sector bureaucracy was unchallenged. In business, "time" is "money." Generally, sales are based on a sales commission and not pay. In the public sector with layers of performance, standards, and in-house promotions, once you are given a pension, social securely, health care, days off, breaks, holidays, vacations basically just show up and do your time. Many people stand in lines; perhaps family members are employed by the public sector and the collective good outweighs the injustice.

If the State-run Motor vehicle were broken up many jobs, wealth and entrepreneurs would be created. Instead a monopoly is allowed to inefficiently serve the drivers of America. The Sherman antitrust act deserves to be implemented and allow business owners to compete with the Department of Motor Vehicle. The State gross income is near a million dollars a week per location.

Chapter 9
Morality

All great thinkers are initially ridiculed – and eventually revered.

- Robin Sharma

Would you live your life differently if you had to leave a legacy? In the 1960s, gestalt therapy entered the parenting dictates of how to raise a successful child. Parents reinforced good behavior and punished bad behavior. Awareness of child-rearing matters based on corroborating experience and research can help create a good environment for the best outcomes while the same size might not fit all. Which comes to an age-old predicament: are we all the same, or are we different?

The reason Donald Trump was elected in 2016 was not his likability, but his relate-ability. He is a common man. He ran against abhorrent phonies that took for their own benefit. The reality is you can take from the system to advance your own interest and deceive yourself that you deserve it, or that if you didn't, someone else would, or that is acceptable because you didn't do anything wrong, the little small lies we justify. But Donald Trump created important jobs for his capable and competent employees and using those strategies created a world-class economy for the American worker. Adults can all participate in the benefit of making all American citizens' lives better. A business owner recognizes that employees count; the business doesn't tell them how to live; The business allows the individual to fit in by what initiative they're going to bring to make the company secure. A reciprocal respect develops between the company and its valued employees who align with the company's vision to maximize competence.

People that give up on work have a low opinion of themselves are less likely to feel satisfied. Typical are lost dreams with a pill to wash away the life of dysfunction, collateral-damage that society pays for. Work makes people pragmatic, efficient, and valued. People want to have a purpose that allows them to feel worthy, speak freely, be happy for others, and ultimately have social mobility.

Rigid and controlling environments suffocate individuality and the ability to stand out as a distinct masterpiece. The balance between self-discipline and autonomy is sensitive to fostering a willingness to conquer achievements, unconditional respect for being flexible, and remaining authentic.

Mephistopheles is my favorite allegorical figure. It is where making a deal with the devil comes from. In German legend, Faust is promised long life, wealth, and beauty if he sells his soul to the devil. You're not free if you are not able to identify your enemy. The devil doesn't tell you how bad it could be for you if you choose those pleasures warned against in the Bible, such as – avarice, vanity, life after death, and temporal pleasures. The human condition gives everyone the same environment as to how an individual is determined by the choices one makes to produce, i.e., good or beget evil. We are born angels, and the environment can corrupt your demise or propel one forward. It is a choice which team will you pick?

The Indian folklore understood it is the spirit within you that you feed that gains your power.

ONE EVENING, AN ELDERLY

CHEROKEE BRAVE TOLD HIS

GRANDSON ABOUT A BATTLE THAT

GOES ON INSIDE PEOPLE.

HE SAID "MY SON, THE BATTLE IS

BETWEEN TWO 'WOLVES' INSIDE US

ALL.

ONE IS EVIL. IT IS ANGER,

ENVY, JEALOUSY, SORROW,

REGRET, GREED, ARROGANCE,

SELF-PITY, GUILT, RESENTMENT,

INFERIORITY, LIES, FALSE PRIDE,

SUPERIORITY, AND EGO.

THE OTHER IS GOOD.

IT IS JOY, PEACE LOVE, HOPE

SERENITY,

HUMILITY, KINDNESS, BENEVOLENCE,

EMPATHY, GENEROSITY,

TRUTH, COMPASSION AND FAITH."

THE GRANDSON THOUGH ABOUT

IT FOR A MINUTE AND THEN ASKED

HIS GRANDFATHER:

"WHICH WOLF WINS?"

THE OLD CHEROKEE SIMPLY REPLIED,

"THE ONE THAT YOU FEED."

Rev. Billy Graham Version

That is why prayer develops an inner voice where your heart is revealed. You allow yourself to become vulnerable and ask for help to correct bad behaviors and ask for new ones. Shedding the old and putting on the new taps into a vibrational rhythm with the universe. The old adage, you reap what you sow, or the Confucian concept of Yin and Yang, the force of self-awareness allows us to purify our lowly nature, and in so doing, we attract that which cleanses our heart, we become renewed.

The Rev. Billy Graham meant when on his deathbed, his last words were, he regretted not spending more time with God instead of futile dinner parties with the likes of Presidents. Is it love or hatred that produces 100,000 million deaths? Christian genocide goes unreported. America was founded on tolerance; the pilgrims settled in a land free to gather without King George III imposing a government religion but freedom to practice with the liberty to worship, follow, and believe without persecution. Somehow, we believe providing shelter to immigrants will absolve the wrong that we refuse to stand up for in the name of genocide.

The immigrants have more Christian predilection than we care to practice. It seems the goal post is constantly moving. Secularism is confronting the lie that it is built on. The founder of the Center for Urban Renewal Education (CURE) recognizes that forsaking core values has morphed into Marxism, where people admonish individual rights laws. Save children from outside our country but kill our own.

Save people who illegally come to our country but forsake the religious liberties we as a nation believe in. Collective taxes from the working class create layers problems despite changing beneficiaries of the poor. As a college student, I applied for an internship with Ronald Regan Presidential office in Washington, DC I was told by the academic Chair of the Political Science Department, "unless I worked for John Kerry, a Senator from Massachusetts or I would not receive an internship." Nepotism is equivalent to Russian Kleptocracy that would take resources or people for the gain of the party. We have become objectified working for the promotion of the party. As a student, I was picked to serve the Democratic Party, and there I would have a career or not advance in politics. Going along with what we don't believe in may put food on the table but marginalizes us. Receiving benefits based on a conditional imperative deprives the individual of moral justification for one's choices. It is tyranny and not a free society that imposes its will.

Can we support the team that lifts us up, or will we hold our head down? The days when a woman married for economics or a man picked a bride to give him offspring is over. Now we must take back the business environment, religious forums, institutions, and government that has strapped us into servitude of class conflict.

Free public education should mean individual self-determination. Health-care options should not be allocated by the privileged few to benefit from; instead, the people intended to receive the benefits in an account that distributes money annually to citizens for the designated purpose it is designed to be used for. The only objection comes from the power brokers who control the resources and hold you down with myths.

The greatest debaters will not engage in hypotheticals. You know why? Because it is not based on fact, it is posed to create fear and subdue. What is in a name? Learning to live label-free is best actualized in Aria's character from the Game of Thrones (GOT) out of many faces being authentic individuality over party.

What is good for the Realm requires a distinguished identity harnessed to achieve reciprocity to ourselves, the family, and the good of humanity. Succumbing to conditioning opens the gates to mediocrity. A life spent fitting in, going along with the pack, and feeling a part of the big group sabotaging your uniqueness. Americans are conflicted between individuality and the mob mentality. Today millennials show their individuality in impressive ways.

Healing themselves through meditative arts and physical group challenges that improve team-building shows the integrative balance to harmony. Practicing good habits of conservation on behalf of the planet protects future generations to come. Raising awareness that disposable plastics cause degradation to the earth, animals, and people. Informing humanity of coexistence between every living man and animal. Animals require a symbiotic environment and are meant to be treated with dignity. So protecting animals from intolerable treatment in circuses so they can enjoy their natural habitats is important. Abuses and crimes of hate have raised the consciousness of offensive intolerances. The work ahead is to include and embrace not alienate. Respect of life all life: babies, animals, nutrition, and exercise, everyone's environment, races, genders, autonomy, trust, and religion will thrive in a capitalist democracy that compassionately shares truth, not domination. (The easy way to change minds, 11212019, pg.C6). (James Walpole in his article "Truth is not a tool for domination, it's a way to connect and share.")

I travel throughout the country with my food products. Selling my wares to the public allows me to observe people and social norms. Recently while working at a state fair, fairgoers knew what to expect from the previous years. Condition as creatures of habit is no better previewed than at a gathering of 180,000 people.

As you should know from reading my book, my mission in life is "purity." The GotMeals label is clean; there is nothing added, only the plant-based ingredients: canola oil, white pepper, and salt. I spent years researching a process to bring fresh and highly nutritious prepared food to market without preservatives. People will tell me to use coconut oil or avocado oil without understanding the taste is restrictive, not to mention nut allergies. Once GotMeals made its message of simplicity and purity clear, I have made a customer for life. I realize that the product attracts the customers for which it was created. Eating healthy ready-to-eat food can mean stepping outside of our lifelong conditioning to accept high amounts of artificially processed food. Surely as we have seen, society pushes forward to improvements which other generations succumbed to as problematic.

The stuffed potato line at the *Eastern States Exposition* in Springfield, Massachusetts, sometimes has an hour-long wait. From my booth, I can see a line form at the stuffed potato stand. If there is no one in line, people walk past the stand. If there is a line, people get in line. It could be raining they don't care, if other people want potatoes, people don't want to miss out. People want what everyone else has. Because people are creatures of popular demand, it is important to raise standards high. Competition is the

American way. That fuel to be the best ignites a free market that wants innovation, better, and faster. Nothing makes a country more successful than a strong consumer. The invisible hand is a theory purported by classical economists signifies that as unregulated free markets bring goods to market at a price, a free-market determines it will bear. In Adam Smith's book "The Wealth of Nations," capitalism was expanded as to what became in 1776, the benchmark of America's virtuous class of producers and consumers.

The avarice of wealth can be achieved, but without prudence will last temporarily. The wealth that is achieved for a means to an end or wealth is preserved for an end to the means. The posterity of one's finance contributes to generations should it be created for a purely unselfish purpose. As money trickles into one's paycheck, consumerism's dangers will deteriorate aggregately, causing self-indulgences to leave a life of toil with little to remember one by.

In *The Wealth of Nations* (1776), Adam Smith described the "invisible hand," a metaphor for the unseen forces that move a free-market economy. When citizens are free to pursue their own economic self-interest, new wealth is created, and unintended social benefits follow, and these benefits are superior to can be achieved by economies that are highly regulated and controlled by a central government.

John Keats, the poet who lived in the early 1800s, is an example of grasping the significance of his purpose. He ditched the medical profession and followed his gift. As a writer, he has blessed generations with penned works to include six poems known as odes, "Ode on a Grecian Urn," "Ode to a Nightingale," "Ode to Autumn," "The Eve of St. Agnes," and "La Belle Dame Sans Merci." He died at the young age of 23. In being true to his purpose, he left a written legacy whose effects are immeasurable even 200 years later.

It creates generational wealth, works of art, advancing scientific works that endure, and shaping society for the better. The choice to exist is simple; a contributor leaves a legacy to improve that time spent in life. Life is for the living, death can be hard to accept, but a life of victimhood needlessly spirals endlessly and consumes with the absence to find pride in oneself. Feminism changed Hollywood's portrayal of women. Thanks to trying to take down a president, if that isn't serendipitous, nothing is. "All good things come to those who wait," and patience really is a virtue. We learn that understanding is a part of the order of the universe. The discernment that is manifested within us is a practice that requires one to, "Flee also your youthful lusts; but pursue righteousness, faith, love, peace with those who call on the Lord out of a pure heart (1 Tim 6:11.) The #MeToo movement annihilated the men's club oath that viewed and treated women as sex objects for decades. Women and men have been compromised by positions of power for long enough.

*Resistance and a quarrelsome person are a red light that distinguishes the guidance given to your spirit as your right to gain enlightenment through a separation from fear, but of power and of love and of sound mind (**2 Timothy 1: 7**).*

The ongoing struggle occurs once we begin to believe we will receive something for free. My Dad would mummer throughout his life, "you think it's easy?!" It could not ring truer than the neighborhood in which I was raised (Environment) had a saying, "Nothing for Nothing!"

There is no other impression that I could attribute to the false come-ons of sale tactics, to wolves in sheepskin (Matthew 7:15). The government deceives everyone by offering benefits to whoever has enslaved the middle-class by taking big Pharma money to pay off the politicians while peddling killer pills to the underserved or rather over-served. Freedom has been preserved by the innocent youth of our military men, forsaking the prime of their lives, laying their precious life down for each person to fight the good fight. My sound advice growing up in an inner-city and watching lives deteriorate caused by drugs and alcohol is don't drink the poison or pay with your life.

A market economy is reflective of those choices pursued by constraint to achieve your individual goals. There is no other world economy that will provide freedom for the overall good of society and ward off corruption than capitalism. The United States is the most powerful nation because it believes in protecting individual fortitude. Will you take your power back? Do you need sound judgment, not confusion caused by a life of reckless disorder? We run from being judged all our life, but in the end, that is the very essence of our existence. No one can judge you but yourself. Knowing who you are, a place where your skills can be developed and utilized by you to capitalize on requires foresight- make a plan.

•Identifying how to capitalize on what you're good at and advocate for yourself.

•Implementing a field of study with an internship to a career path or utilizing skills that are income producing

•Allocating long-term financial security

•Family planning is imperative and begins with choosing the attributes you want in a partner for life.

Don't follow the empty promises of a corrupt world that will rob you of your individual autonomy in the name of social justice. Your tangible and intangible rewards will be glandered by your stealthy persistence to delay temporal gratification for the prize of individual fulfillment.

Putting your trust in another individual comes in many forms. It could be a recommendation to take a course with a well-regarded professor, and it could be asking for help when traveling on where to visit. Trust also is listening to a newscast or social media influencer. Facebook may seem to have provided "Snoops" for assurance or is blind faith in Facebook's CEO declassifying what it doesn't want you to know. Funny, we could go through an education system and become desensitized to messaging. Ask yourself if maybe you were receiving information that had an agenda.

Provide below is a quick reference to some clear agendas that causes harm to freedoms eroding liberty by the branches of government we trust to protect us.

• The Slaughter House, Easter Sunday in 1873 Republicans and Blacks were surrounded by anti-black militia intending to not only kill them alive inside but murder anyone who escaped out a window. Those who would have been convicted used their power and connections to compromise the Supreme Court to change a few laws even to prevent Congress from having a say.

• Chicago handgun ban violated the Second Amendment, but the Supreme Court again changing the "Due Process Clause" to "substantive due process" contrived to take away gun rights. This injustice occurred Under the Franklin Roosevelt administration.

• In the 1930s, the government permitted the courts to seize food that farmers grew using the Commerce Clause. Designed to create a dependency on big government. Instead of giving food boxes to citizens, they got social services.

• After marijuana was legalized in California, federal agents used the Interstate Commerce Clause to punish medical marijuana growers. A legislative effort to regulate conditions to collect revenues.

• In 1967, using the search and seizure Judges, law enforcement and bureaucrats changed the law trying to convict based on evidence the plaintiff felt was obtained with unreasonable search and seizure. In later years many crimes could be solved with "reasonable" expectations of a per son's privacy, as seen in computer and cell phone evidence.

• 1973 Norma McCovey, a 23-year-old who was given the pseudonym "Roe" was conveniently exploited by legislatures in a scheme to push an agenda to end unwanted pregnancies. She spent her next 37 years trying to save mothers recognizing that she was a pawn in the horrific decision to end human life[15].

The media is no longer indifferent; it, too, has been compromised. Today, news and talk shows are used to create

---

[15]Magnet, M. (2019). Clarence Thomas, and the Lost Constitution, Imprimis, Vol. 48, Number 9. Retrieved from: https://imprimis.hillsdale.edu/wp-content/uploads/2019/09/Imprimis_Sept_8pg_web.pdf

controversy to increase viewership inculcate political agendas in unison with selling advertising. Subjecting yourself to manipulation empowers the enemy within to take your power silently.

In conclusion, the goal is to encourage the reader to choose your time on this planet carefully, block the negative, and soon you will only think in colors of the rainbow and pursue authentic habits sewing, drilling, playing guitar, traveling, operating computers, planning startups, studying finance, and so forth. It will lead you to individual success and intended self-worth. It is not arbitrary or by being born of nobility that you can achieve happiness – it is by virtue and hard work to build a life beyond what your given that will endure for generations.

Alas, you can say to yourself,

"I have fought the good fight, I have finished the race, I have kept the faith."

1 Cor. 9:24-2 nm7

Chapter 10
Man in the mirror

Have you ever set goals?

It feels exhilarating when you think about accomplishing your goals and achieving the things you dream about. Doesn't it? However, there is one drawback when it comes to making your dreams come true. The problem with goals and pursuing your life with the focus required to accomplish your goal is that it allows our desire for approval to compromise our self-reliance.

Doing things by way of recognition, not doing things of your own volition, causes one to sacrifice your own independence of being authentic. The desire for permission sometimes means that you have to wait for someone else's approval. An example of someone else's permission makes us wait for the job application that we applied for did we get it? Are we good enough? It's always by somebody else's standards even in a social setting the initiation of Greek life on campus, or the social consternation of Facebook or YouTube recognition is measured by the number of followers if it's always dependent on someone else's wanting what you have, which limits one as creators of their dream. Yes, you may call it a goal, but will the achievements contribute to your internal satisfaction and your overall meaning that remains true to your identity. There comes the point where I truly believe that doing things that are qualitative (excellence) not qualifying (seeking approval) can propel us where we are capable of organically going in life.

Our new world presents multiple platforms; political, economic, social, individual, educational, religious and in all representation, one must engage in authentic conversation allowing for compromise to reach a common goal for individuality, happiness, fulfillment, and satisfaction to pursue, be heard (support), and actualize one's destiny.

Doing what you do best can set you free. In other words, the importance of excellence can be fostered by environmental recognition, aka are rewards, money, status, or it can be organic. However, less common it can manifest in the great masterminds Steve Jobs, Satoru Iwata (Nintendo), Jeff Bezos, developers of quantum mechanics, biogenetics, and artificial intelligence alter science and the way we live.

Include the sacred guidance and human wisdom below – if you should ever get lost, it will straighten your path.

Ten Commandments

- Love God most of all
- Use words pleasing to God
- Keep Sunday holy
- Honor your parents
- Do not harm anyone
- Be faithful to your husband or wife
- Do not steal
- Always be truthful
- Do not be jealous
- Seek simplicity
- Frank McCourt in his book "*Teacher Man*," would add
- No Lying
- No Cheating
- No Stealing

- As a New York Teacher raised in a famine in Ireland, he ingrained within his students the standards of
- No Whining
- No Complaining
- No Excuses

The dynamic of individuality with a collaboration of both environmental and organic influencers is unique to each person. Mainly recognizing one's strength comes from within and staying authentic means not to be changed by societal norms or conform to a status quo. This distinctive approach has preserved the entrepreneurial fervor to excel and not to be controlled in a socialist or state-run government but to allow one to evolve for the single power of PURPOSE!

My life journey that culminates my paradigm began on a family vacation to the USSR in 1979 when the country extended visas to offer Americans a view of Russia. The drinking water was treated with so many chemicals we had to drink boiled water or *chai* often. I still try to impress my Russian friends with the only phrase I grasped, *Ah diem chai, pagalsta* (pass the tea, please). My family knew the problems drinking soda caused to deteriorating the enamel on teeth and a host of other health issues; needless to say, we were a sugar-free soda house back in the USA, but in Russia, it seemed the healthy choice for us. The young adults inside the country feared the KGB secret service was following them.

Materialism could not be rationed when they saw the Americans walking in those dungarees, "Please sell your jeans to me, or my girlfriend will leave me!" That desperate plea propelled my family to engage in black market denim profiteering. One day a week, the commissary would open for purchasing household needs. Families received bread and things until the goods ran out.

Everything ran out there was no infrastructure or supply chain. The people looked old in dark-colored layered clothes, and girls held arms when they walked together. Lenin was the treasure of the visit. His tomb guards were admired with changing of the guards, as people passed by in reverence. School children saluted a framed picture above the chalkboard chanting allegiance to their country. The militaristic setting provided a sense of security. The children's allegiance was to their state school, not their families. Accountability for their academic performance and excellence came from state standards, not their families or their personal yearning to excel. Tours consisted of museums, schools, ballet, parks, and monuments. The stories of Stalin – his palace gardens and architect – burnished his legacy even to visitors. While the people live with nothing, Lenin built timeless grand water parks to distract from the reality of human suffering. The citizens lived a futile life in contrast to Americans. One could believe we had opportunities to live like kings and queens.

I may have had the advantage of recognizing that America had become too familiar to cherish opportunities that other countries would die to have. We have become ungrateful for the opportunity to own a Bible, read a Bible, and the freedom to worship. The church serves to welcome all who wish to pray, unlike the Communist countries that restrict anyone from going into a boarded-up, closed church. Communism has no God; the state is the God of the people. Secular oppression replaces creation in textbooks with Darwin's design. The claim purports that the homo sapiens bones his expedition discovered in Australia were theorized to explain how the world began. This indoctrination separated science from faith. The apparent agenda used to influence mass allegiance to austere state conformity. I lost my bearings in the confusion of realizing the lies used to control societies. I lost myself for years as I imagined all types of indoctrination clashing with the individual would cause. You will conform or not belong. Into my adult years, I processed my purpose despite organized hypocrisy, but because of the exposure that I have had traveling changed my political awareness. The one place I felt understood was in a higher universe. I joined intense bible study groups, listened to radio evangelists, and drew closer to transcendental thought that operative in self-acceptance. Traveling to the farthest parts of the earth, I have shared church services with people of nearly every race and nationality. Which I had on my bucket list since my adolescence and still church hop to this day.

It always seems the people who have nothing materially have what is of greatest value: God. I met a man giving a lecture. He thought that because I read the same books he read, that our paradigms were aligned. He said, "Religion is the root of all war." Well, who likes war? I thought. But our God is about a personal relationship. The religious part requires we affiliate with a spiritual conviction guided by the

Holy Spirit and act rationally upon our choice. We have the freedom to go wherever we want, not so in many parts of the world- where religious persecution prevents an epistemological growth. It would be equivalent to voting for a political party because of free cigarettes, a warm ride, and a few minutes of caring qualified the bad guys for winning power. I have given you the resources to determine if you want to play along with a fantasy that the government will take care of you.

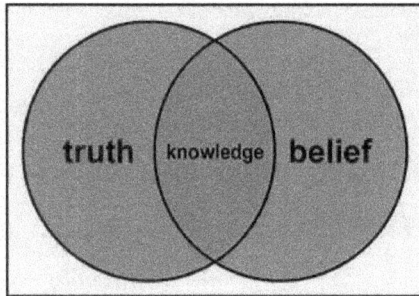

You will always know if you are being worked over – when God is removed, votes are bought, books don't come home from schools. Dependence on government services creates more dependency – food is not nourishing, city-dwelling is preferred to land ownership, the government rations health care, one side is the unity that glues you to the next comrade.

Expand your mind – travel far and wide, give of yourself – that which is deemed genuine. Issues such as climate change, women's right to end a life, equality, sex, drugs – they're not all the same, and the subtle distinction requires you to think and discuss in an environment with no hidden agenda. The days are over when true freedom of speech is accepted: "group think." Dispelling wordplay by an awareness that sex, drugs, and rock and roll are not the same. Some knowledge comes with time. If you were to ask the 1970's generation, now in their 60's if they would repeat, believe, or follow the slogan preached by inculcation. It is my experience knowing what they witnessed that "drugs" kill.

It is similar to the millenniums believing marijuana is recreationally therapeutic. What it does is numb you taking away the best years of your life until ten years at a time pass by, and you have made no individual growth and accomplishments are fewer. This is difficult to identify, but games, i.e., Fortnight Pokémon or Call of Duty, have preoccupied an entire generation from their youth. It is a possession of one's soul. It steals your days, returning nothing in exchange. Staying on track means you need to check in – how does what you're doing serve you? Honest conformation is challenging accepting and making a plan to replace bad habits with good ones. Discuss options with someone that can be a trusted counsel. Enjoy being a challenge and challenge those that challenge you, take risks, and absorb experiences before you form a position. As the government grows, public sector jobs grow. I have never seen anyone co-dependent on government services amass wealth and freedom or break the cycle of government corruption.

The elites raise taxes yet inherited their wealth from the people, go ahead, try to take it from them. They will never give anything back that they took. Instead, they live lavishly with excesses while controlling the goal post, in government, media, academia, and the issue of the day.

Do you know why a poor man never got rich? Do you think it was because there was a party in the United States that didn't want to help? No, it is because the "power" you give away keeps you conflicted, living in guilt. The Clintons and Obamas make this point too easy. They blame Wall Street and "greedy" corporations. Hard work creates money, jobs, and wealth for everyone. It is the pot calling the kettle black. The elites are guilty of taking money from hard-working people all to advance their privilege, make the restrictive laws and rhetoric to suppress any competition. If you are a proponent of Capitalism or Socialism – both give away their wealth to benefit society. We no longer can use the money to solve problems that harm millions of lives and don't benefit the intended recipients.

The government budgets relying on padding annual budgets with a "use it or lose it" approach promotes disguised wealth for the elites to fund their greedy schemes. They don't play fair. You are the frog as the proverbial heat is turned up in the pot, it's too late when you realize you're in boiling water. It is the same analogy for our youth intentionally being dumbed down with rewritten civic textbooks, addictions, and social approval. It is too late until you realize the party has ended.

The future will bring greater individuality, unlike with the most common "oneness" the status quo methods Marxism could not account for technological advancements such as homeschooling, internet, chatrooms, artificial intelligence, and health care. The consciousness of the world has changed mainly caused by a pandemic plaque of 2020. Information is being broken from the distortion of the evil network; the hidden enemy is losing power as objective reality demystifies conditioning. New technology no longer conforms to the censored disinformation. Being ridiculed at the office or fitting in at the party is no longer shaping social discourse. The usurping of power is being dismantled. The time is vital, allowing individuals to readjust from the past subversion by media conglomerates that intentionally control all the local and cable news to influence a false paradigm. Simply put – no one is free when they're being programmed and unable to make an accurate, informed decision. How we discern and judge what is reality from illusion reminds me of King Solomon.

The king was presented with two who both had recently given birth. One women's baby died in delivery. They stood before the king claiming the baby belonged to each of them, but only one could have been the true Mother. The king had to decide too, who appeared to be the Mother. Since everything is not always as it appears, his challenge would rely on wisdom. Unlike the media, the king had no reason to mislead the women for his own advantage other than reputation. He would forever be known as the wisest man that ever-lived King Solomon. He agreed to cut the baby in half. One of the two women screamed – "No, give her the baby!" The king made his decision. The wise king said the baby does not belong to the woman holding the baby. The rightful Mother unselfishly gave her child life instead of being killed (1 Kings 3: 26-28).

America will be strong with healthy marriages, strong family, principles that inspire, courtesies that put your fellow man first, and support unbiased truth. Release your chains – no man is a slave. If you are to choose with no prejudice, the power-hungry academic unions, would not have to control children's minds with deception or adults with skewed loaded stories to cause emotional compliance.

The day of free markets has been snuffed out in every country in the world. The last thread of hope is you. It is inherent to human nature to function relationally. Belonging to something greater than ourselves has been manipulated by imposing ideologies through "groupthink" and replacing individualism beaconing one to a higher power, freely. It is your choice to choose coercion or self-determination. The opposite of Love is fear, law-order vs. chaos. Free vs. exploited. The best example is protecting the nation that welcomes all far and wide to the inalienable protection under the constitution Life, Liberty, and Justice for all. Babies' rights are being subverted to advance science in stem cell research or disguised as family planning, or health care, or a women's right to her body, but every election a new slogan is rallied to unite women together against a group that wants to save the babies. Women are liberating themselves through independence despite the deception. Goodness will win as a kinder nation to protect life for babies and the environment. Inner cities are rallying for education change through school choice.

A robust economy creates jobs to ensure social services for the disabled, elderly, and need. Access to holistic health care, better food, and exercise improves caring for ourselves, providing an alternative to big pharma. Saving money creates wealth. It is about practicing self-control, denying yourself the pleasures, and delaying gratification to build a future of self-reliance. Based on these principles, I believe the man in the White House should be a conservative that has control in their own lives to be frugal. The State governor should also be conservative to hone in expenses. However, the municipality can be a direct reflection of the residence and the values that they embrace. The conversation that everyone must contribute benefits to those who, by their own demise, will not work is upsetting to the middle class. Everyone deserves to work because idle time is the devil's playground. Immigrants come with dreams of work, work that we cannot get our own citizens to do. Government programs perpetuate a false sense of security.

What would the indigent do if they had nothing but themselves to rely on? They would stop wasting time and work for their pay. The party is over, and you can't spend all day hanging out with all your friends, losing your mind and inhibition, and expect to get things hard-working people work for. It is not fair to take from others and contribute nothing in return, making except for making you dependent on subsidies.

In the food business, we rely on manual labor, usually foreigners or DACA recipients, who already receive welfare subsidies and disability. They asked me, the employer, to keep their wages under $800.00 or some amount under the social service program minimum income or their government income would end. Eventually, I could no longer manage to hire, train, and contribute to the bizarre scam. I was being asked to concede my business taxes, both local and State, as my business became a pawn in their entitled perception of gainful employment. Does the government understand people deserve to earn as much as they can? This is a perfect example of how too much government is harmful. Take, for instance, Sue, she honestly makes $16,000, but if she can show what she earns, she can produce double that. She doesn't need to receive food assistance, fuel assistance, utility assistance. Programs that enrich society are designed to create ownership.

Self-sufficiency is demonstrated by using your money to spend. It is the power within the American Dream to be a responsible, good steward – a proud owner. Bring the disenfranchised living under the forces of marginal expectations and fraction incomes into the light of full citizenship, fully competent to contribute, and count as having a significant purpose of being reckoned with.

Minimum wage is a noose around work production, value and must be advanced to change with equal pay for all. The living standard for each household should be fifty-thousand. Children receive health and education accounts set up with proof of conception, an ultrasound image, and accounts activated upon birth. The family paid leave is a right given to value human worthiness. Every parent deserves the opportunity to bond with their loved ones. Every family deserves vacations. All work and no play make productivity become dull – go get refreshed. Handouts devalue humanity. The opposite is evident in sports by rewarding goals that benefit the team. Who do you want on your team: a player who wins or has no ambition to get the job done? You want someone dependable, honest, and creative that brings value! Imagine living in a community that rewards citizens for cleaning up the local park or pick up strewn recyclables.

Pay for work in the most innovative ways for people to contribute the best they can. With the advent of cell phones, individuals can earn extra money by snapping a picture of the community improvement and reap the benefit of income. A recyclable program would give the green voices a solution to get paid not for what they say but by being the solution.

Everyone can recycle garbage and get paid per pound. A photo would validate per bag payment, and the picture would get sent to an employer, and the like-kind "Pay it forward" would take on a whole new benefit. Let people feel important, don't penalize them – encourage them. Doing good inspires others; it will be infectious. Who would complain to pay taxes for the benefit of community enrichment work programs? Tax should be collected to benefit citizens, not policyholders. As a business owner, I am reminded to pay sales taxes every month and annual entity taxes regardless if that month's losses exceeded sales; the bills must be paid. I am discouraged by the lack of honor attributed to corporations in the USA. The big old government will be the only game in town too big to defeat, too big to do the right thing, and what will be lost forever is the individuals that make up the fabric of American businesses.

The dynamic of individuality with a collaboration of both environmental and organic influencers is unique to each person. Mainly the ability to recognize one's strength comes from within and to stay authentic mean not to be changed by societal norms or conform to a status quo. This distinctive approach has preserved the entrepreneurial fervor to excel not to be controlled in a State-run government but for the single power of PURPOSE!

I live in a liberal town. Over the years, I have seen innovations merge to solve social emancipation. Entitlements were used to provide a way into housing, education, work programs and while those have been positive like anything the negatives are drug use, playing the system, unethical bureaucratic benefiting from other people's money, low skilled workforce, reliance on incompetence and loss of hope, loss of ambition and loss of self-determination.

There is a saying; everyone is a liberal when they're young or don't have the money yet. It's only when they look at retirement savings do they become Republicans. Giving away your money for someone else to give away has never changed society for the better – not in America, not in any country. The rule of economics is that it's easy to spend someone else's money. An example is property tax. Why would someone drive a new expensive car only to pay an exorbitant amount of taxes that is self-imposed gluttony?

The innate disincentive is punishment for working hard. But then a drug dealer blaring loud lyrics can be heard as their shiny expensive Mercedes waits at a city street traffic light. What comes easy goes easy. Invest in forever. The implications are drastic – the consequence of materialism is a trap causing one to end in debt while one who saves is unscathed. I once asked why prices in areas of poverty were higher than elsewhere? The answer was to make up for the pilferage. In the end, we all pay. In Florida, there are expensive cars encouraged by the removal of property tax. The removal of a tax liability encourages everyone to have nice things instead of punitive laws enforcing a status quo.

Municipalities can elect not to impose a property tax. The economic value stimulates newer, expensive motor vehicle purchases. The State benefits from the sales tax, and the local government become less inclined to fund social programs that they created in the first place.

My Jewish friend told me that if you want to live long, get an Indian doctor, if you want to win a legal battle, hire an Italian lawyer, but if you want to be rich, hire a Jewish accountant. Saving money is hard when people don't have extra money to invest. Technological programs developed brokerage firm apps, i.e., Webull, Robinhood, and Charles Schwab, make learning the markets understandable for all who wish to learn. Developers specifically created a brokerage app to encourage stock investing called "fractional investing reducing the amount of money needed to buy into a stock. It is a good time to be a part of the economic landscape.

"The greatest force in the world is compound interest."

-Benjamin Franklin

Education

The State uses education and health care to disenfranchise children and adults. An education review was designed to empower students instead of school boards that collude funds away from per-pupil monies. Public education and health care program are full of deceit. The Health care that is designed to protect children from parents giving the State authority in what is known as HIPPA.

Unmasking the deception will allow the people to take back power for their families. One such organization is the Student Education Empowerment (SEE), which would allow a transparent curriculum giving students the ability to inform the oversight board if politics are being used to influence young minds.

SPARK started in Camdenton, Missouri, by a group of kids that organized a similar coalition known as Students Protecting All Rights for Kids. Their mission is to get every school free of political intolerance and end subtle or overt indoctrination. In Charles Mackey's book, "Extraordinary

Popular Delusions and the Madness of Crowds raises awareness of "the herd" effect, and it's destructive effect compounding anxiety resulting in a 20-year high suicide among youth.Social justice is not delivering equity for all. It is killing because children need to be promised the government stays away from implementing mind control among unsuspecting citizens. Politics that prey on the young is like a bully that picks on the little guy, we shout, "pick on someone your own size." Pokémon fights with equal power to subdue the opponents.

But what if all could RESPECT one another. In 1990 the toppling of the Berlin wall liberated elections, prisons, free speech, commerce, markets, press, education, and thought took many years to follow. Ingrained beliefs do benefit the few, those controlling the narrative- the powerful that point the fingers at an enemy, are the enemy. Today, Germans, Russians, Ukrainians, Cubans, Venezuelans, Chinese, etc. are all around to engage in a conversation. To learn other beliefs first, you must be open, as Gorbachev promised in "glasnost." It is hard to let go of rigid beliefs take, for instance, the children the Taliban used to weaponize against the American and Israelis. Both countries practice no harm.

\The Israelis would build around an anthill, to adhere to the principle of Zionism. There is a house for everyone on the other side for every good deed, and the Mitzvah doesn't go unnoticed – you are the carpenter who builds the house you want to spend in for eternity.

I began this book by telling you, "We all tell white lies some time in our life" – maybe for fear of reprisal, maybe to fit in, maybe the truth hurts to admit. The path to a true you begins the moment you realize you are in control. Did you ever hear the saying, "It is what it is"? It means: Deal with it. Most of the time, we lose our sense of value traded for seeking the approval of others. Let them deal with it! For you, the only person who inspires the universe is a straight shooter. We can only get there by being authentic. We refuse to react; it is never said better than to "just be."

> ### THE MAN IN THE GLASS
> by Dale Windrow
>
> When you get what you want in your struggle for self,
> And the world makes you king for a day,
> Just go to a mirror and look at yourself,
> And see what the man has to say.
> For it isn't your father, your mother or wife,
> Whose judgement upon you must pass;
> The fellow whose verdict counts most in your life,
> Is the one staring back from the glass.
> Some people may think you are
> a straight-shooting chum,
> And call you a wonderful guy;
> But the man in the glass says you're only a bum,
> If you can't look him straight in the eye.
> He's the fellow to please, never mind all the rest,
> For he's with you clear up to the end;
> And you have passed your most dangerous,
> difficult test,
> If the man in the glass is your friend.
> You may fool the whole world down your
> pathway of years,
> And get pats on the back as you pass;
> But your final reward will be heartache and tears,
> If you've cheated the man in the glass,

My Mom gave me a poem as I crossed the metaphoric bridge from indifferent teen to self-aware young adult. When she left us, I gently placed the poem back in her casket. An updated version poignant meet a cataclysmic catastrophe called the Wuhan virus beginning January 06, 2020 for my family as We entered Hong Kong China. It since claimed lives by spreading worldwide. Somehow society gets directed back to the person inside of themselves. Self-consciousness is the voice of assurance that pushes us to grow many times we become numb without daily reflection.

An Imagined Letter from Covid-19 to Humans states the reason awareness is like oxygen.

Stop. Just stop.

It is no longer a request. It is a

mandate.

We will help you.

We will bring the supersonic, high

speed merry-go-round to a halt

We will stop

the planes

the trains

the schools

the malls

the meetings

the frenetic, fury rush of illusions and "obligations" that keep you from hearing our single and shared beating heart,

the way we breathe together, in unison.

Our obligation is to each other,

As it has always been, even if, even though you have forgotten.

We will interrupt this broadcast, the endless cacophonous broadcast of divisions and distractions,

to bring you this long-breaking news:

We are not well.

None of us; all of us are suffering.

Last year, the firestorms that scorched the lungs of the earth

did not give you pause.

Nor the typhoons in Africa, China, Japan.

Nor the fevered climates in Japan and India.

You have not been listening.

It is hard to listen when you are so busy all the time, hustling to uphold the comforts and conveniences that scaffold your lives.

But the foundation is giving way,

buckling under the weight of your needs and desires.

We will help you.

We will bring the firestorms to your body

We will bring the fever to your body

We will bring the burning, searing, and flooding to your lungs

that you might hear:

We are not well.

Despite what you might think or feel, we are not the enemy.

We are Messenger. We are Ally. We are a balancing force.

We are asking you:

To stop, to be still, to listen;

To move beyond your individual concerns and consider the concerns of all; To be with your ignorance is to find your humility, to relinquish your thinking minds and travel deep into the mind of the heart; To look up into the sky, streaked with fewer planes, and see it, to notice its condition: clear, smoky, smoggy, rainy? How much do you need it to be healthy so that you may also be healthy?

To look at a tree and see it, to notice its condition: how does its health contribute to the health of the sky, to the air you need to be healthy? To visit a river, and see it, to notice its condition: clear, clean, murky, polluted? How much do you need it to be healthy so that you may also be healthy? How does its health contribute to the health of the tree, which contributes to the health of the sky, so that you may also be healthy? Many are afraid now.

Do not demonize your fear, and also, do not let it rule you. Instead, let it speak to you – in your stillness,

listen for its wisdom.

What might it be telling you about what is at work, at issue, at risk, beyond the threats of personal inconvenience and illness?

As the health of a tree, a river, the sky tells you about the quality of your own health, what might the quality of your health tell you about the health of the rivers, the trees, the sky, and all of us who share this planet with you?

Stop.

Notice if you are resisting.

Notice what you are resisting.

Ask why.

Stop. Just stop.

Be still.

Listen.

Ask us what we might teach you about illness and healing, about what might be required so that all may be well.

We will help you, if you listen[16].

---

[16]Flyntz, K. (2020). A Message From the Virus, or Our Ancestors? Psychology Today. Retrieved from: https://www.psychologytoday.com/us/blog/bear-in-mind/202003/message-the-virus-or-our-ancestors

We inevitably get old with age and comes a breath of perspective.

If you're lucky enough throughout the journey of life, you will look into the mirror and like the person looking back at you. May the inspiration within this book allow you the altruism in your old age when all your loved ones are gone to find you content to sit with yourself on your front porch with a cup of tea sharing the highlights of your life with the next generation, "the passing of the torch," is a life worth its weight in gold.

A Book and a Jar – My most successful counseling sessions addressed the client's fears, anger, mistrust, phobias, bad habits with a jar. The instructions are:

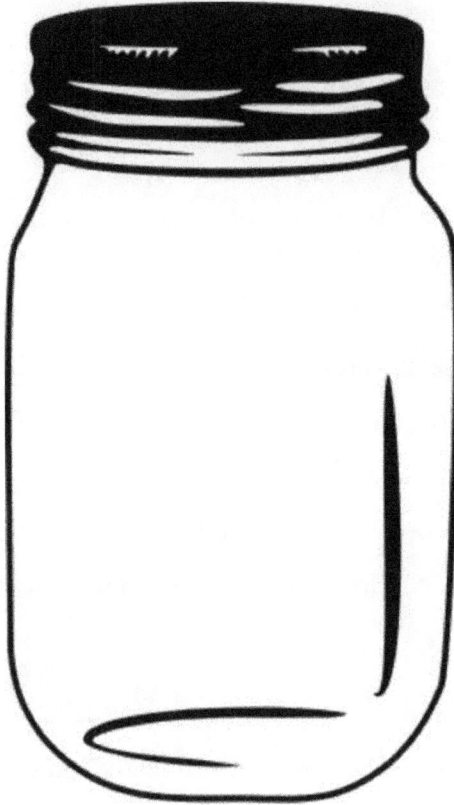

Anytime you feel negative thoughts to write down what you are experiencing on a piece of paper.

Then take the paper and crumble it, open the jar and put it in the jar, and put the top back on to seal it in there.

Now anytime you want to visit your problems, they will be in the jar.

In the next session, I would ask my clients if you visited the jar since last week. No-one ever revisits their problems – of course, they may add other pieces of crumpled paper with new problems, but they're over it once they know where they can find it suddenly it disappears. The best way to confront a problem is to acknowledge it.

I have given you a book for introspection

A jar for problems

Whenever you react to anyone by gossiping or spew negative words – write post-it labels and put it on the jar.

Apologize to the universe to redirect bad behavior and increase wellness.

Just as a firefly, you are free to shine bright in the darkness. Don't put yourself or allow anyone to put you in a jar – radiate!

LABELS BELONG ON JARS